Transition and the Spatial Organization of Industries

European University Studies
Europäische Hochschulschriften
Publications Universitaires Européennes

Series V
Economics and Management

Reihe V Série V
Volks- und Betriebswirtschaft
Sciences économiques, gestion d'entreprise

Vol./Bd. 3047

PETER LANG
Frankfurt am Main · Berlin · Bern · Bruxelles · New York · Oxford · Wien

Alexandra Schleier

Transition and the Spatial Organization of Industries

The Case of the Bread Industry in the Irkutsk Oblast, Russia

PETER LANG
Europäischer Verlag der Wissenschaften

Bibliographic Information published by Die Deutsche Bibliothek
Die Deutsche Bibliothek lists this publication in the Deutsche Nationalbibliografie; detailed bibliographic data is available in the internet at <http://dnb.ddb.de>.

Zugl.: Bonn, Univ., Diss., 2003

D 98
ISSN 0531-7339
ISBN 3-631-52424-2
US-ISBN 0-8204-6588-7

www.peterlang.de

Abstract

The present study addresses the question of how the spatial organization of the bread industry in the Irkutsk Oblast changes under the conditions of the Russian transition economy.

In a theoretical discussion the spatial organization of the bread industry in a planned economy, a market economy and a transition economy in the same regional setting are derived. The discussion concludes with hypotheses on three issues that describe the change of the spatial organization of the bread industry: 1) The course of transition: It is expected that old enterprises remain in the market while a large number of new enterprises emerge. The diffusion of new bakeries over space is determined by two mechanisms: in rural areas agricultural enterprises are hit by price liberalization and face the subsequent gap between input and output prices. One way to react is vertical integration, which includes bakeries. The second mechanism is a normal spatial diffusion through the settlement hierarchy. 2) The enterprise population: Three types of bakeries are expected to emerge: small businesses, agricultural enterprises that produce bread for their workers and agricultural enterprises that produce bread for the market. 3) The market structure: The bread industry is a locally fragmented industry. Hence, different types of markets are expected to develop. In large settlements where old bread plants are located the structure of a dominant firm with a fringe will emerge. In other settlements monopolies, duopolies or oligopolies will emerge according to the settlement size.

The comparison of the number of enterprises before and after transition showed that a large number of new enterprises has emerged. For the analysis of the diffusion process a model was constructed that combines the two abovementioned mechanisms. The comparison with the actual course of diffusion shows that the predicted and observed curves are almost identical while differences between the observed curve and the normal epidemic diffusion model are obvious. The analysis of the enterprise population clearly revealed the market orientation and non-market orientation of the enterprises respectively. The new enterprises were classified in a cluster analysis. Unexpectedly, only two groups of enterprises were detected that could be clearly assigned market oriented and non-market oriented enterprises in all indicators. Furthermore, the behavior of the old bread plants showed that the degree of competition from new small enterprises has had considerable impact on their adjustment towards markets. The analysis of markets showed that most of the non-market oriented enterprises are located in rural areas in a monopoly position, while most of the market oriented enterprises are located in oligopolies or in competitive markets with a dominant firm. Neither a relation between market size and market structure, nor a relation between price and market structure could be established. However, distance was revealed as an important determinant of the absence or presence of an enterprise in the market and of the price level in the markets.

It can be concluded that markets have partly developed. While markets have developed in urban areas that are distant from the center, in urban areas near to the center the absence of new bakeries hints of barriers to entry that might be related to connections between the administration and the old bread plants. Where new small bakeries have entry to markets they play an important role in the adjustment processes of the old enterprises. The exception is the development in peripheral rural areas where, due to demonetization, a functioning market does not develop.

Zusammenfassung

Die vorliegende Studie beschäftigt sich mit den Veränderungen in der räumlichen Organisation der Brotindustrie der Irkutsker Oblast unter den Bedingungen der russischen Transformationsökonomie.

In einer theoretischen Diskussion wird die räumliche Organisation der Brotindustrie in einer Planwirtschaft, Marktwirtschaft und Transformationswirtschaft für dieselbe räumliche Situation abgeleitet. Die Diskussion schließt in Hypothesen zu drei Aspekten der Veränderungen in der räumlichen Organisation der Brotindustrie: 1) Der Verlauf der Transformation: Es wird erwartet, dass alte Brotunternehmen im Markt bleiben während eine große Zahl neuer Unternehmen entsteht. Die Diffusion neuer Bäckereien in der Zeit und durch den Raum wird durch zwei Mechanismen bestimmt. In den ländlichen Räumen werden landwirtschaftliche Unternehmen von der Preisliberalisierung und der daraus entstehenden Schere zwischen Input- und Outputpreisen getroffen. Eine Möglichkeit darauf zu reagieren ist vertikale Integration, die auch Bäckereien einschließt. Der zweite Mechanismus ist der typische Diffusionsvorgang durch die Siedlungshierarchie. 2) Die Unternehmenspopulation: Es wird erwartet, dass drei Typen von Unternehmen entstehen: Kleinunternehmen, landwirtschaftliche Unternehmen, die Brot für die Versorgung ihrer Arbeiter produzieren, und landwirtschaftlichen Unternehmen, die Brot für den Markt produzieren. 3) Die Marktstruktur: Die Brotindustrie ist eine lokal fragmentierte Industrie. Entsprechend wird erwartet, dass sich verschiedene Typen von Märkten herausbilden. In großen Siedlungen, in denen alte Brotfabriken ihren Standort haben, wird sich die Struktur einer dominanten Firma mit einem Gürtel kleiner Unternehmen herausbilden. In anderen Siedlungen werden entsprechend der Größe Monopole, Duopole oder Oligopole entstehen.

Der Vergleich der Anzahl von Bäckereien vor und nach der Transformation hat gezeigt, dass eine große Anzahl neuer Bäckereien entstanden ist. In einem Model zur Untersuchung des Diffusionsprozesses wurden die beiden oben genannten Mechanismen kombiniert. Der Vergleich zu dem tatsächlich beobachteten Verlauf zeigt, dass die vorhergesagte und die beobachtete Kurve fast identisch sind, während die Unterschiede zwischen einer typischen Diffusionskurve und der beobachteten Kurve offensichtlich sind. Die Analyse der Unternehmenspopulation zeigt deutlich die Marktorientierung oder Nichtmarktorientierung der Unternehmen. In einer Clusteranalyse wurden die neuen Unternehmen klassifiziert. Anders als erwartet wurden nur zwei Unternehmensgruppen identifiziert, die jedoch gemäß aller Kriterien eindeutig als marktorientiert bzw. nicht marktorientiert bezeichnet werden können. Weitherhin kann am Verhalten der alten Brotfabriken abgeleitet werden, dass Konkurrenzdruck durch neue kleine Unternehmen einen großen Einfluss auf die Anpassung der alten Unternehmen in Richtung von Märkten hat. Die Analyse der Märkte zeigt, dass der Großteil der nicht marktorientierten Unternehmen im ländlichen Raum in einer Monopolstellung lokalisiert ist, während die meisten marktorientierten Unternehmen eine Position in Oligopolen oder Wettbewerbsmärkten mit einem dominanten Unternehmen einnehmen. Es konnte weder eine Beziehung zwischen Marktgröße und Marktstruktur noch eine Beziehung zwischen Preis und Marktstruktur hergestellt werden. Es zeigte sich jedoch, dass Distanz ein wesentlicher Faktor für die Existenz oder Abwesenheit einer Bäckerei in einem Markt darstellt, sowie einen Einfluss auf das Preisniveau in einem Markt hat.

Abschließend läßt sich folgern, dass sich zum Teil Märkte entwickelt haben. Während in urbanen Gebieten, die sich in größerer Distanz zum Regionszentrum befinden, Märkte entwickelt haben, deutet das Fehlen neuer Bäckereien im Regionszentrum auf Eintrittsbarrieren hin, die in Verbindungen zwischen Oblastverwaltung und Management alter Brotfabriken gefunden werden könnten. Wo neue kleine Unternehmen Zugang zum Markt haben, spielen sie eine wichtige Rolle für die Anpassungprozesse der alten Unternehmen. Eine besondere Situation herrscht in peripheren ländlichen Räumen, wo sich aufgrund der Demonetarisierung keine funktionierenden Märkte entwickeln.

Table of Contents

List of Tables

List of Figures

Appendix 2

Abbreviations

APK	Agroprommyshlenniy kompleks (Agricultural production complex)
CIS	Commonwealth of Independent States
Goskomstat	Gosudarstvennyi komitet po statistike (State Committee for Statistics)
Gosplan	Gosudarstvennyi planovyi komitet (State Planning Committee)
HI	Herfindahl index
IET	Institute for the Economy in Transition
IO	Industrial organization
R&D	Research & Development
SME	Small- and medium-scale enterprises
SOPS	Soviet po isutsheniyu proisvoditelnykh sil (Council for the Study of Production Forces)
TPK	Territorialnyi prommyshlennyi kompleks (Territorial production complex)
Transsib	Trans Siberian Railway
ZEF	Zentrum für Entwicklungsforschung

Acknowledgements

I would like to extend my sincere gratitude and appreciation to my first supervisor, Professor Dr. Joachim von Braun, for his inspiring and motivating ideas that accompanied my research at the Center for Development Research (ZEF). Grateful thanks go also to my second supervisor, Dr. Peter Wehrheim, for continuous discussion and support.

I owe very much to Professor Natalia Syssoeva at the Institute for Geography, Irkutsk, for facilitating the successful conduct of the enterprise survey and helpful comments on the current research. I thank Professor Vashanov at SOPS for interesting discussions and helpful insights into the realities of the Soviet planned economy. Further thanks for helpful comments go to colleagues at ZEF, the Institute for the Economy in Transition (IET) and at the Institute for Geography, Irkutsk: Dr. Arnim Kuhn, Dr. Susanna Wolf, Dr. Shyamal Chowdhury, Dr. Sergey Dudenko, Dr. Pavlovich Mosunov, Dr. Natalia Rogovskaya, Natalia Korzennikova, Professor Eugenia Serova and Dr. Irina Khramova. Finally, I would like to thank my family, my friends and colleagues, all those who helped me through encouragement and moral support

1. Introduction

1.1 Background

What has been happening and is still happening in the countries of the former Soviet Union is usually given the name transition. This term is defined as 'the set of reforms and the timing and sequencing of reforms with which a country implements the system switch from plan to market'[1]. In the countries of the former Soviet Union the systemic change was an expression of dissatisfaction with socialism. When the reforms started, enormous improvements in people's lives were expected.

However, it takes effort to implement a new political and economic system and, hence, implementation has reached different stages in different countries[2]. While the reforms in Eastern Europe are regarded as successful and advanced, though not complete, the public looks baffled at the developments in Russia and other countries of the CIS. Despite success stories, regular reporting on corruption, poverty, demonetization and subsistence production show that transition has proved to be a complicated and unforeseeable process. What has been neglected in the idea of transition is that implementing a market economy does not necessarily mean eradicating structures stemming from a planned economy. Moreover, the new rules and norms pre-determined at the federal level have to be transferred down to the regions and individuals which requires learning and adjustment processes. Given the complicated circumstances, these adjustments were not always in the direction of the intended market economy but produced certain transition-specific survival strategies, not least that the creation of the market framework was not always in the most capable hands[3]. The result is an economy, which is ruled by different regimes. This is the starting point of the present dissertation. The Russian economy is understood as a mixture of market economy elements, persistencies of planned economy structures, and phenomena specific to the transition economy[4]. These transition phenomena could lead to other forms of inefficiencies in the economy and prevent reallocation in such a way that inefficiencies

1 Wehrheim, 2002, p. 1 (forthcoming).
2 World Bank, 2002.
3 Aslund, 1999, p. 3.
4 Chavance & Magnin, 1995.

remain. One source of inefficiencies that was identified by agricultural economists and geographers but has gained less attention in the transition debate is the spatial organization of industries[5].

The spatial organization of industries is a result of economic factors. As the decision processes of the planned economy have failed to allocate efficiently, it can be expected that the spatial allocation has also been inefficient and that transition will lead to reallocation. Geographical issues have been addressed by economists in the transition context covering enterprises of a huge variety of branches and regions[6]. This approach neglects two important aspects: Firstly, the organization of industries is specific to branches and, subsequently, is the spatial organization. Hence, reallocations over space can better be described by observing single industries. Secondly, the development of entrepreneurship from below, i.e. the role of new small and medium sized enterprises (SMEs), is crucial for the development of functioning markets[7]. The role of SMEs in the development of markets can better be studied with the example of a single industry.

Figure 1-1 indicates how the concepts of transition and space are connected. However, the graph represents the idealistic understanding of transition as a switch. The right-hand side shows planned economy, the left-hand side shows market economy. The arrows indicate how the different levels, federal, regional and local, are connected to each other. On the planned economy side, all arrows start at the centre. The planner whose allocation rationale is cost minimization, as shown in the ellipse, determines allocation of production factors and goods. The regions do not have a function in the allocation process despite serving as an instrument to channel investments. Firms at the local level are economic actors in the sense that they fulfil the directives and plans of the center. As a result, the spatial organization of the economy and of single industries is shaped by the decisions of the central organs.

With the implementation of the necessary conditions for building a market economy, price liberalization, decentralization and privatisation, the relations between the different levels change considerably. The arrows now indicate an interrelationship between the federal level and the local level as well as between the regional level and the local level. Market institutions have to be built at federal and regional levels that are in compliance with the ideas and necessities of the economic actors, i.e. households and enterprises. Regions gain influence through their regional policies that can foster or hamper the progress of reforms and

5 Kurzew, 1996; Wandel , 2001, pp. 38-40; Stadelbauer, 1997, Shaw, 1999.
6 Brown & Brown, 1998.
7 Roland, 2000, p. 7.

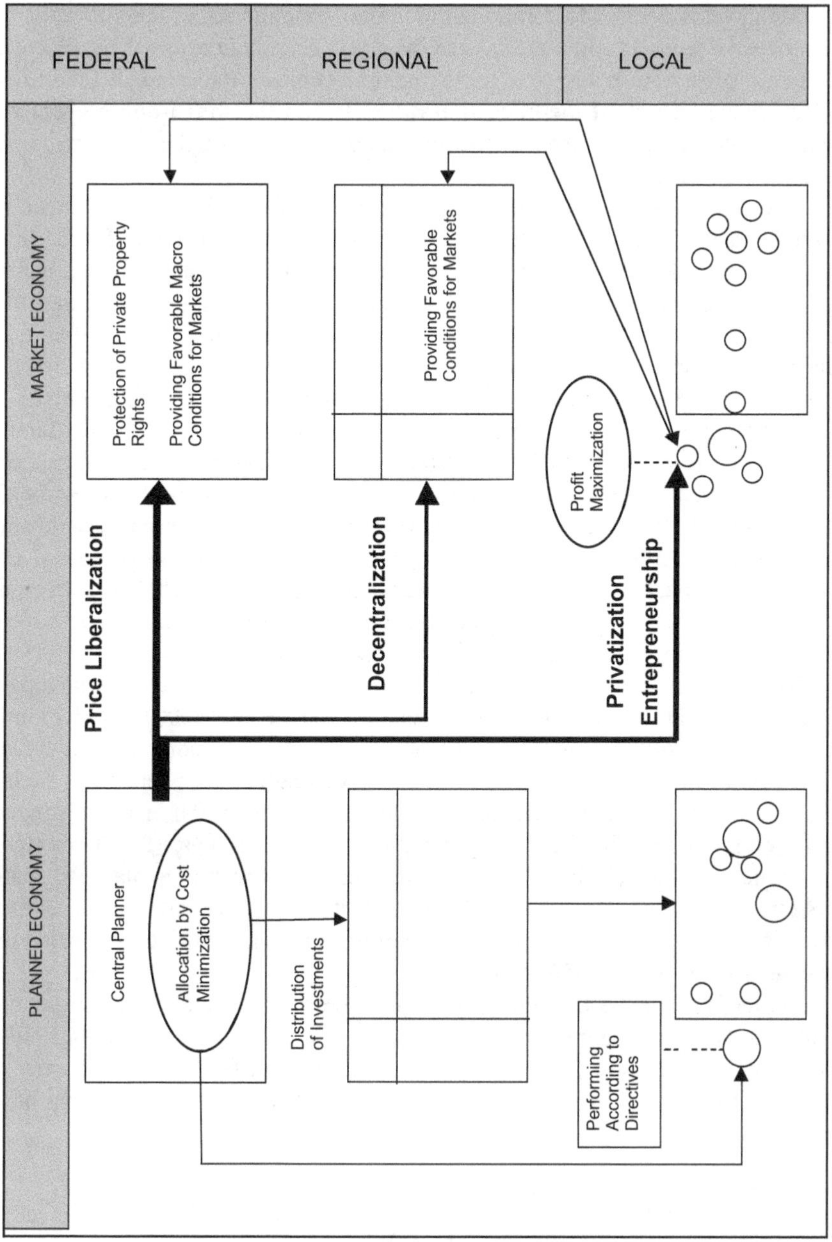

Figure 1-1: Aspects of Spatial Reallocation During Transition

market development[8]. Most importantly in the economic sense, the allocation decisions have shifted from the center to the single economic actors. The allocation rationale of private enterprise, profit maximization, is indicated in the ellipse. Through the change of the allocation rationale and the shift from the center to private enterprise, a change in the spatial organization of the economy is expected.

The spatial organization could be described through all levels, national, regional and local. However, here the focus lies on the organization of a single industry as indicated in the lower part of the figure. The industry depicted is a regionally fragmented industry and the pattern of location changes during transition by the entry and exit of units as well as by the growing and shrinking of units. In the idealistic view of transition the system change can be approached by comparative static analysis and economic theory provides the respective models.

Although space has a long tradition in economics and the names of famous economists are connected to it, it has fallen into oblivion in mainstream economics for a long time. The renaissance of space in economics started in the beginning of the 1990s initiated through writings by Paul Krugman and was given a clear image in 2000 when Fujita, Krugman and Venables declared spatial economics to be mature for a publication with textbook-like character[9]. However, the book represents only one view out of various views on space. It is possible to identify basically three strands of space and economics.

The question of the first strand is: Where does economic activity take place and why? This is the introductory question of Fujita et al. (2000). The real interest behind this question is to explain the concentration of economic activity at a few locations, i.e. the existence of urban agglomeration and phenomena such as manufacturing belts and areas of agricultural production. Though a distinction between sectors can be found, for example in urban economics for the existence of textile cities and financial cities, the models do not seek to explain the spatial organization of single industries. Rather they focus on the economy as a whole consisting of two or more sectors (agriculture and manufacturing) and being distributed over a number of regions.

While in this class of models strategic interactions of enterprises are exogenous, they are endogenous to the second class of models. Their question is 'What is the optimal location for an enterprise or production facility?' The former focuses on the shape of the spatial pattern, the latter on the spatial behaviour of the enterprise.

8 McIntyre, 1998; see Melyukhina & Wehrheim, 1996 for an overview of agricultural policies and their impact on market development.

9 Fujita et.al., 2000.

During transition, as mentioned above, new economic rules have to be implemented by single economic agents, i.e. enterprises and households. Since in studies of transition the implementation at this level and the new entry of enterprises has gained less attention, this study leaves the first class of spatial models and concentrates on the second.

All models in the second class of spatial models have in common that they focus on the behaviour of single agents while still being very different in nature. The first type belongs to the classical location theory based on the writings of von Thünen, (1875), Weber (1929), Christaller (1933), Lösch (1940) and Isard (1954). Ghosh & Rushton (1988) provide an exhaustive literature review on location allocation models, which can be regarded as successors to location theory. The models are of a more practical nature and represent a methodology to find the optimal location for a facility. A huge range of models has emerged based on variations in the number of facilities to be located and in the assumptions on the distribution of demand. They have found broad acceptance and application in the siting of facilities like hospitals, emergency services, schools or fire departments[10]. The target variable of the optimisation problem is regularly the minimization of transportation measured in time or money spent, or distance travelled. The idea of efficiency[11] can be applied to this type of model in the following way. The difference between a one-point economy and a spatial economy is the necessity to transport raw materials to producers and final products to consumers, which, in technical terms, employs resources. Given the fact that this resource utilization is inevitable, transportation minimization would determine the efficient spatial system. The amount of transportation is defined by the size and number of production units. Economies of scale emerge as a driving force since the productivity of production units is defined by their size. The system would be efficient when the gains by economies of scale offset the losses by transportation. This description reflects the technical definition of productive efficiency, since costs in these models are not related to prices of goods. The location allocation models solve the problem of a planner in a centralized command type economy. They are applied in market economies basically for the siting of public facilities, i.e. for governmental institutions whose prices, if any, are usually fixed and where the target is to provide the population with the service for the lowest cost.

The other type of location model comes from a completely different direction where the interest lies not on spatial structures but on the structures of markets,

10 Felder & Brinkmann, 2002; Hancock, Holden & Swales, 1991; Martin & Williams, 1994; Sasaki & Kuhisina, 1995.

11 For the discussion of efficiency in the context of location allocation models see Parr & Swales, 1996, 1999.

i.e. from industrial organization. In each textbook for industrial organization some pages are spent on the Hotelling type of location model. However, mentioning them derives not from an interest in location but from a very specific problem in industrial organization. For the definition of markets the homogeneity of products is crucial although it is virtually impossible to find perfectly homogenous goods, because quality creates differentiation; but location also can create differentiation. Two otherwise completely homogenous goods can be differentiated simply by the fact that they are sold at two different locations. In such a spatial economy the consumer incurs transportation costs to get the product. Consequently, the actual price of a good is the selling price plus transportation costs – again measured in time, money or distance. In this case the problem for the enterprise is either to find the optimal location or the optimal price. In the models presented, the location is usually fixed because equilibrium becomes impossible when location is variable. Most of the models concentrate on the optimal price given the price charged by other enterprises and their location, the distribution of the consumers, and the enterprise's own location[12]. The problem is formulated as a profit maximizing function under the assumption of a certain market structure.

Under these circumstances individual enterprises decide on their location and performance, and the rule by which they decide is profit maximization. In a spatial economy where all costs other than transportation costs are independent of the location and where homogenous production technology is assumed which allows all units to produce at the same marginal cost, transportation cost minimization would again apply since there is no scope to influence the price, and all costs except transportation costs are independent of the location. In this case no spatial price differentiation for the sourcing of raw materials exists and no spatial price discrimination[13] for the marketing of products is realized. In their presence the situation changes considerably and becomes much more complex. Regardless of spatial price discrimination, spatial price differentiation on the input side is most likely to exist in reality. Because total costs are relevant for the profitability of the enterprise, the opportunity to purchase raw materials at a much lower price at a location more distant than the alternative source for inputs can considerably reduce the role of transportation costs as a factor for location. Here the economic concept of efficiency applies.

The two types of models described above provide the theoretical background to the present study as the former can be assigned to a planned economy and the latter to a market economy. However, as already stated, this comparative-static

---

12 Shy, 1998, p.149.; Tirole, 1998, p. 279.
13 Cheung & Wang, 1995; Eber, 1997.

approach is too simplistic and has to be adjusted for the distortions that occurred during transition.

1.2 Task of the Dissertation

It has become clear in the preceding explanations that the study focuses on the spatial organization of a single industry and the changes that are occurring during transition. Though theoretically the idea of transition is understood as a switch, in the analysis the distortions that emerged during transition have to be fully accounted for. Furthermore, it is the intention to focus on the role of new entrepreneurs in the development of markets. Hence, the industry chosen for the analysis has to meet certain requirements. The industry must be such that the entry of new entrepreneurs can be expected. Consequently, naturally concentrated industries have to be excluded. Additionally, the industry should be locally fragmented in order to achieve enough observations of markets. Transition-specific phenomena should be well developed in the industry and, finally, data collection should be feasible.

The bread industry fulfils these requirements. In countries with a comparable bread culture it is spatially fragmented and the number of enterprises is usually large and composed of a huge number of small bakeries and a small number of industrial producers. Furthermore, bread is a very important component of Russian nutrition and one of the least elastic goods[14]. Hence, even under conditions of transition, a complete breakdown of the industry due to a lack of demand cannot be expected. Transition phenomena are very distinct in the agricultural sector and, consequently, in the sectors linked to it[15].

The study is located in the largest transition country, the Russian Federation. However, the conditions of data collection in the Russian regions make it necessary to limit the study to a single region. Secondary regional data is not centrally available and requires travelling to the regions. Regarding the region to be chosen, the most important factor is that the industrial pattern of the bread industry existing at the beginning of the transition was mainly shaped during the planned economy era. This can best be found in Eastern regions as economic development had started in the European part of Russia and reached the East only relatively recently.[16]. Out of 89 Russian regions, 33 are situated east of the Urals. To best account for an economic structure stemming from a planned economy and

14 Compare chapter 2.4.
15 Compare chapter 3.4.
16 Compare chapter 2.2.

for the peculiar situation of Siberia, a vast area, a region of the Eastern Siberian Economic Raion has been chosen, the Irkutsk Oblast.

Hence, the task of the present dissertation is to analyse the changes in the spatial organization of the bread industry in the Irkutsk Oblast, Russia. To better handle the task, research questions have to posed. The basic question can be formulated as

How did the bread industry of the Irkutsk Oblast adjust during transition?

Figure 1-1 indicates that changes in the location structure can occur through exit and entry of enterprises, which at the same time changes the enterprise population. This is given if the management of old enterprises has undergone the adjustment process and set its goals accordingly, and if new entrepreneurs take profit opportunities, in other words: a market economy has been implemented. The result would be a change in the enterprise population and subsequently in the location pattern. From this follows the sub-question:

a) Has the enterprise population changed during transition?
b) What were the reasons for the change, market forces or other factors?

If transition-specific phenomena lead to distortions in the development of markets, it is expected that the locations of market-involved enterprises and non-market-involved enterprises reveal a regular spatial pattern. The questions follow:

c) Where have markets developed and where have markets not developed?
d) How can the resulting pattern be explained?

1.3 Organization of the Dissertation

The **second chapter** of the dissertation will give an overview of the economy of the Irkutsk Oblast and the role of the food economy in the regional economy to explain where the observed bread sector is imbedded.

At the beginning of the analysis it has to be explained why and where changes are expected and what the implications are for the enterprise population, the location structure and market development. This is the objective of the third chapter. **Chapter three** first describes the spatial allocation process of the bread industry in a planned economy, and second, the spatial allocation process in a market economy. From this discussion reference configurations for the bread industry in a simple regional setting are derived. The comparison of the reference configurations which gives the expected changes is adjusted for distortions caused by transition phenomena, which are explained in a third subsection. The results of the discussions are summarized in hypotheses on the course of transition in time and space, the enterprise population after ten years of transition, the market structures and prices.

According to the hypotheses, **chapter four** analyses the course of transition in time and space. The analysis is theoretically based on a diffusion approach that sees market economic behaviour expressed in opening and operating a bakery as the innovation in the region. Two overlying diffusion mechanisms are presumed that are combined in a model on diffusion, which is then compared to the actual diffusion process. A regression analysis on the determinants of the diffusion process completes the chapter.

The results of chapter four already indicate the distortions that occurred in the emergence of market-oriented enterprises. **Chapter five** is dedicated to a thorough description of the enterprise population and particularly of the new enterprises with special respect to market orientation. To do this, the new enterprises are grouped on the basis of a cluster analysis. Subsequently, the clusters are described and compared to each other and to the old enterprises.

While chapter five focuses on the characteristics and behaviour of the enterprises, the objective of **chapter six** is to analyse their organization in markets. The number of markets is compared to the number of municipalities and the Herfindahl index is calculated for the existing markets. The combination of different types of enterprises within the markets is studied and regularities are identified. The determinants of the existence of a market and of the respective market structures are analysed in a regression analysis.

Chapter seven discusses the results of the analyses following the question: 'How much market has developed?'.

1.4 Data

The present study is based on three sources of data. For the description of the planning process and the allocation decision, unstructured interviews were conducted with experts of the Council for the Study of Production Forces (SOPS) at the former GOSKOMSTAT. The experts worked as planners for the development of the agricultural production complex (APK) during the Soviet era and could provide detailed information on the allocation rationale and malfunctioning of the system. Furthermore, SOPS provided access to plans and materials on methodological issues.

Official statistical data and data provided by the Oblast administration were used for the analysis of the bread sector of the Irkutsk Oblast. It has to be noted that, although enormous amounts of official data are available in Russia compared to other countries, the reliability of the data has to be questioned. Particularly in the economic sphere, there is regular underreporting by enterprises. Examples of this can be found in table 1-1 and chapter 2.4. Consequently, the analysis relies on secondary data where necessary.

The basic source for the analysis is an enterprise survey that was conducted in July and August 2000. As the aim of the analysis was to study the entire bread industry and as the expected number of observations was relatively small, it was intended to survey all bread baking facilities in the region. However, due to reasons of feasibility, some of the districts in the region were excluded. The regional coverage is shown in figure 1-2. The excluded districts belong to the Far North region, which is still subject to special regional policies. In these regions climatic conditions are extreme and population density is extremely low. Due to a lack of accessibility the survey did not cover seven districts out of the 33 where 6,4 per cent of the total population in the Oblast live and 3 per cent of the bakeries are located.

The interviews were prepared according to information obtained from the Oblast administration. As the figures in table 1-1 reveal, the number of bakeries observed in the survey and the number reported by the administration differ considerably. In most of the cases the observed number is higher than the reported number. The number of bakeries that declined to answer is low (around 4 per cent) and is representative of the number of bakeries in each district. Hence, the database is representative of the total population of new bakeries. However, the total population listed here contains only the businesses that were identified by the interviewers during the survey with the help of the district administration. Though the district administration turned out to be very well informed in contrast to the Oblast administration, it is possible that some bakeries were overlooked.

Concerning Soviet bread factories, the official statistics report 19 plants. One large plant is located in a district that was not covered by the survey. Out of the 19 plants 10 gave answers to interviewers. In addition to the newly founded bakeries and the old factories, 32 bread baking units were identified by the interviewers with the help of the Oblast and district administrations that are older than 1992 and belonged to a support system mainly in rural areas. These units were surveyed together with the new bakeries. For these units the same rule of representation in the database applies.

Figure 1-2: The Irkutsk Oblast: Districts Covered by the Survey

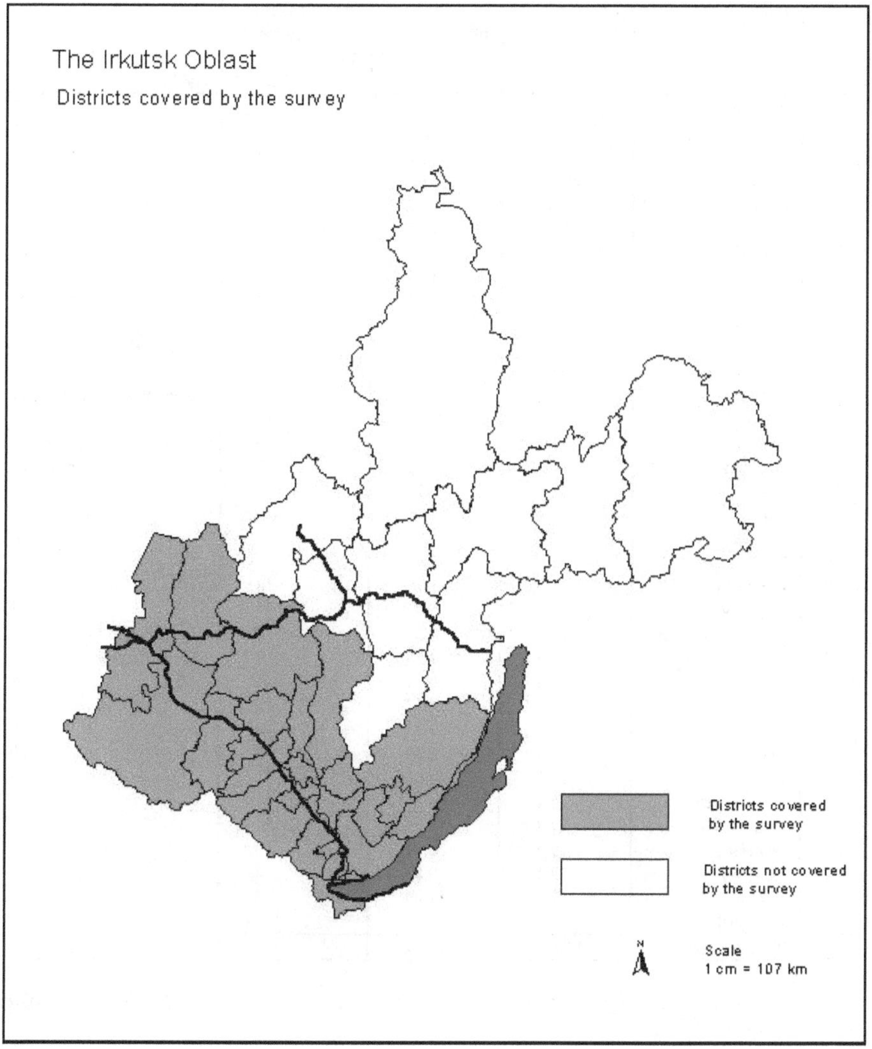

Source: author's own drawing

Table 1-1: Population and Number of Bakeries in the Raions of the Irkutsk Oblast

	Raion	Population 1.1.2000 In 1000	Population in percentage of the total	No. of bakeries named by the Oblast administration	Observed Bakeries, foundation 1992 and later
1	Angarskiy	281.2	10.23	2	3
2	Balaganskiy	10.7	0.39	5	3
3	Bodaybinskiy	30.9	1.12	0	0
4	Bratskiy	347.5	12.65	5	13
5	Zhigalovskiy	11.1	0.40	2	Excluded from the survey
6	Salarinskiy	35.2	1.28	4	5
7	Siminskiy	97.9	3.56	5	11
8	Irkutskiy	645.3	23.48	6	9
9	Kasavchinsko-Lenskiy	25.3	0.92	0	Excluded from the survey
10	Katangskiy	6.2	0.23	0	Excluded from the survey
11	Kachugskiy	23.2	0.84	6	2
12	Kirenskiy	26.9	0.98	1	Excluded from the survey
13	Kuytunskiy	41.5	1.51	11	11
14	Mamsko-Chuyskiy	12.0	0.44	0	Excluded from the survey
15	Nizhneilimskiy	71.9	2.62	2	Excluded from the survey
16	Nizhneudinskiy	87.6	3.19	1	23
17	Olkhonskiy	9.3	0.34	7	0
18	Slyudyanskiy	47.0	1.71	0	0
19	Tayshetskiy	94.5	3.44	1	22
20	Tulunskiy	31.9	1.16	12	24
21	Usolskiy	160	5.82	4	3
22	Ust-Ilimskiy	128.9	4.69	0	Excluded from the survey
23	Ust-Kutskiy	70.5	2.57	0	Excluded from the survey
24	Ust-Udinskiy	17.8	0.65	1	1
25	Cheremkhovskiy	123.7	4.50	12	19
26	Chunskiy	47.5	1.73	4	8
27	Shelechovskiy	65.5	2.38	3	0
28	Alarskiy	28.9	1.05	11	17
29	Bayandayevskiy	15.1	0.55	10	8
30	Bokhanskiy	27.9	1.02	9	11
31	Nukutskiy	19.5	0.71	10	3
32	Osinskiy	22.4	0.82	4	6
33	Ekhirit-Bulagatskiy	30	1.09	6	10
	Total Irkutsk	2748.0	100%	144	212

Source: Survey 2000, Information by the administration, Committee for State Statistics of the Irkutsk Oblast, 1997.

2. The Economic Structure of the Irkutsk Oblast

2.1 Introduction

The study region is situated in the center of Siberia, which as a whole is characterized by extreme low population density. Defining the territory east of the Urals as Siberia, it can be stated that 75 per cent of the territory of the Russian Federation lies there and approximately 30 per cent of the population live there. The population totals 31,5 million people, who are distributed over 26 regions. With 2.7 million people, the Irkutsk Oblast is one of the most populated regions in Siberia and in the Russian Federation. This number of people on a territory of 768.800 km² results in a population density of 3.5 persons/km², which illustrates the general situation in Siberia[17]. However, given the enormous north-south extent of the Siberian regions, this indicator is not very informative. Most of the population is concentrated in urban centers in the south. The statistics for the Irkutsk Oblast show 14 cities and 80 per cent of the population as urban. Eight of these 14 cities lie along the Trans Siberian Railway. The picture becomes even more distinct by calculating the percentage of the population (as at 1.1.2000) in the cities of Irkutsk (593,700), Angarsk (269,900; 30 km distance from Irkutsk) and Usolye Sibirskoye (103,500; 45 km distance from Irkutsk), which adds up to 35 per cent of the total population[18]. Beside the center around Irkutsk and the settlement belt along the Transib, a second center exists with Bratsk in the North-West of the region and is connected to Irkutsk by railway and by waterway.

This distribution pattern reflects the economic development of Siberia that was based on cheap energy and natural resources. These endowments and its location in relation to Asian markets give it a favorable position among the Siberian and Russian regions.

17 Goskomstat, Statistical Yearbook 1999, CD-ROM.
18 Committee for State Statistics of the Irkutsk Oblast, 1997, pp.7-8, 12.

Figure 2-1: The Irkutsk Oblast. Districts and Main Communication Lines

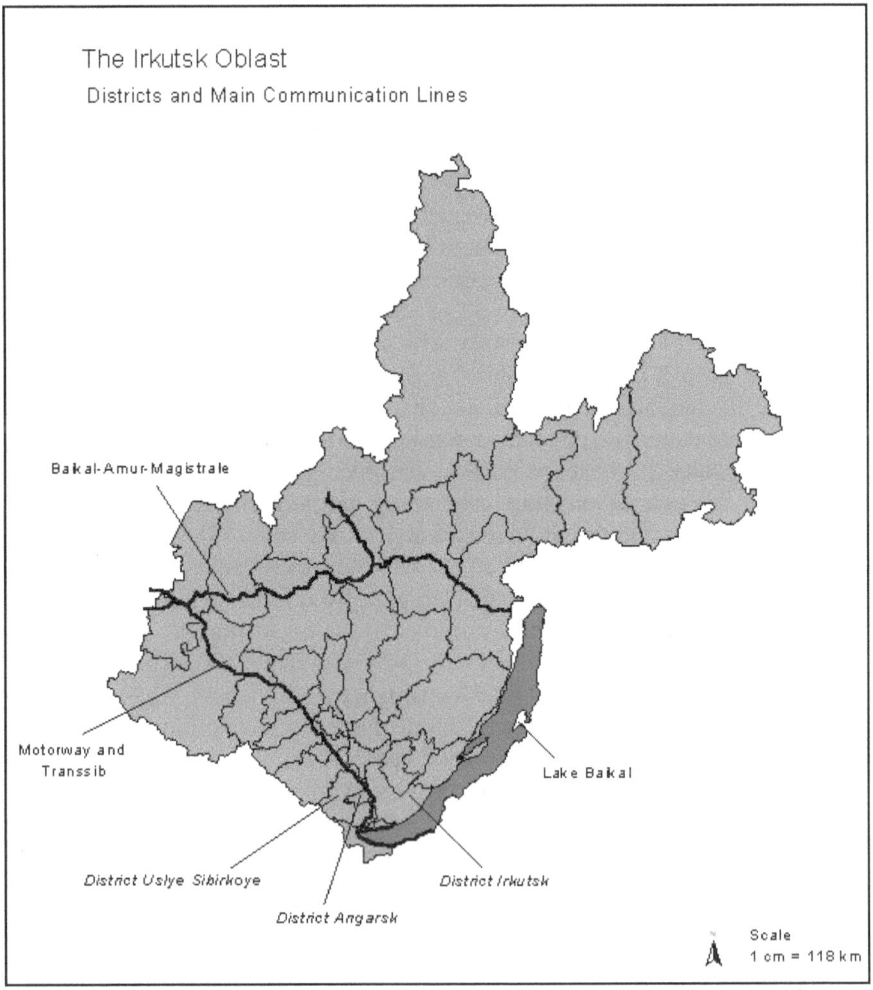

Source: author's own drawing

Figure 2-2: Population Density in the Irkutsk Oblast

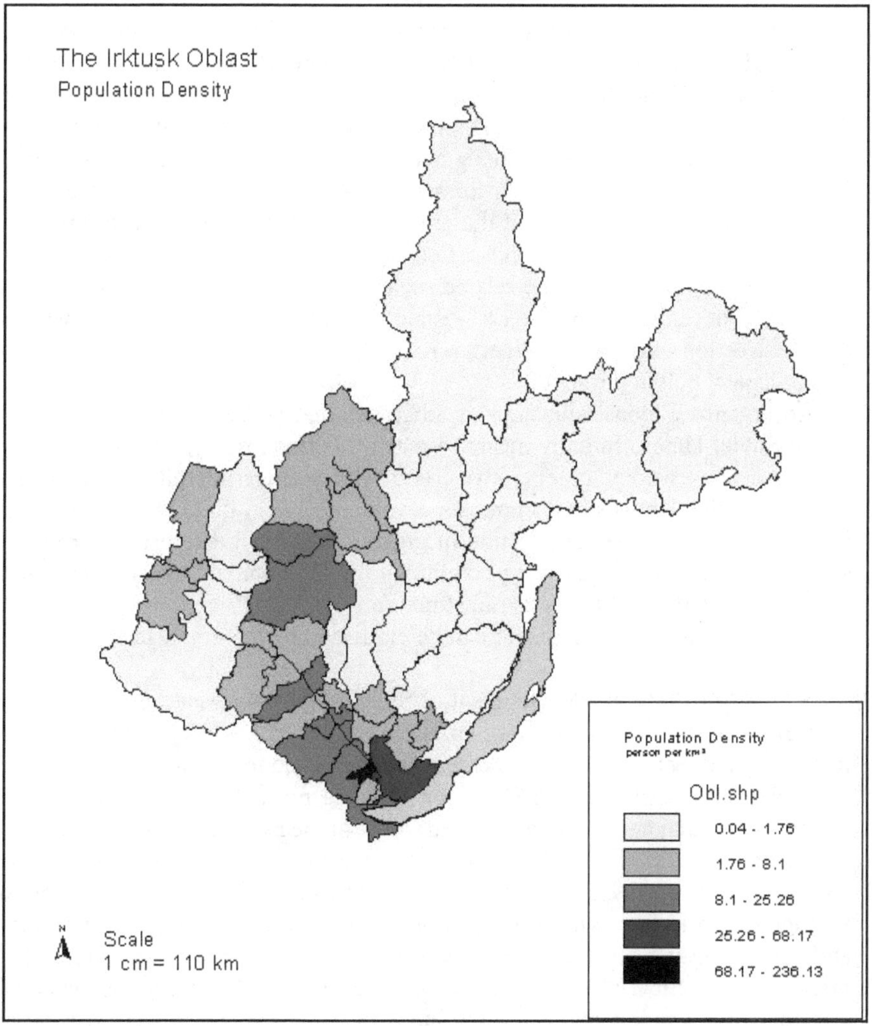

Source: Committee for State Statistics of the Irkutsk Oblast, 1997, author's own drawing

2.2 The Historical Development of Siberia and the Irkutsk Oblast

As shown in different sources,[19] Siberia has the image of being the colony of Russia. This originates in the fact that a high share of the natural resources of Russia and the Soviet Union are located in this region and, moreover, in the fact that the rulers made use of these resources without showing any respect for the rights and needs of the people living and working in the region. In tsarist times Siberia served as accommodation for an overflow of prisoners and as a supplier of metals for coin minting. Until the middle of the 19th century, such mining as was developed represented islands of economic activity in this vast area. There was no development of an interrelated regional economy. The first decision crucial for the development of Siberia was a consequence of Russian gold fever, i.e. the construction of the Trans Siberian Railway, which led to the development of the settlement belt in the south[20].

An organized industrialization of Siberia started with the first five-year plan of the Soviet Union. Initially meant to make Siberia another America by means of autonomous worker co-operatives, and with a short interplay of integrated planning during Khrushchev's time, its development very quickly became what it is now famous for: the construction of gigantic industrial enterprises and power stations at the cost of the living conditions for the population, economic infrastructure and a diversified industrial structure.

This unbalanced development can be explained by the organization of industry in the Soviet Union.

Starting in 1955, the development of Siberian industry went through the concept of territorial production complexes (TPK), for which huge construction enterprises were responsible. These enterprises belonged to so-called branch ministries. Hence, constructing a TPK meant building not only industrial enterprises but also the social and economic infrastructure in the respective region. However, as the enterprises were judged by their successes in developing resource extractive industries, they regarded plants for manufacturing industry as small disadvantageous projects and made little effort to build up consumer goods industries and supporting industries[21]. These branches did not have their own construction organization in Siberia. Though there was a Ministry for Food Supply, the development of food supply and consumer industries could not keep pace with the industrialization. The same was true of housing and social infrastructure. The researchers in the central planning institutes saw these deficiencies, but they were

19 Forsyth, 1992; see the writings by Vladimir Rasputin.
20 Klueter & Giese, 1990a; Grigoryeva, 1983.
21 Klueter & Giese, 1990b; Lifanchikov et al., 1983.

not able to do much more than make recommendations. The planning dedicated to a co-ordination of industries at a regional level also had very limited influence.

As the development of the settlement structure witnesses, the Irkutsk Oblast is a representative example of these policies. Though Irkutsk as the Paris of Siberia was already a famous outpost of Russia in Siberia in a very early stage of colonization (freedom of the city 1686), and two other towns appeared in the 18th century, the urban statistics show very clearly the importance of Soviet policy for the region. All other urban settlements were founded after 1917. In 1917 Sima and Cheremkhovo were founded along the Transsib based on coal mining, in 1925 Bodaibo in the Near North based on gold mining, and Usolye Sibirskoye. Between 1927 and 1949 three other towns emerged, again along the Transsib[22]. The enormous population growth between 1939 and 1989 (200 per cent), as well as the relation between rural and urban population as depicted in figure 2-3, confirm this development.

Figure 2-3: Population Growth and Distribution in the Irkutsk Oblast between 1939 and 1997

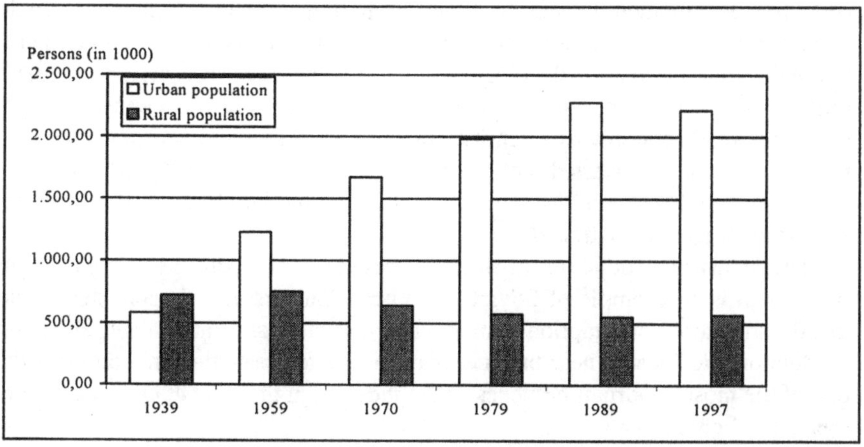

Data Source: Committee for State Statistics of the Irkutsk Oblast, 1997, p. 5.

22 Committee for State Statistics of the Irkutsk Oblast, 1997, p. 7.

2.3 The Economy in the Irkutsk Oblast

Particularly important for the economic structure of the Oblast are the foundation of the cities of Angarsk (1951) and Bratsk (1955) as both are examples of the particular Siberian development[23].

The second world war played a crucial role in the diversity of the industrial structure. To protect industrial production, the Soviets undertook enormous efforts to relocate industrial enterprises from the European part of Russia to Siberia. As many of them belonged to the machine building industries and consumer goods industries, it contributed to a more diversified economic structure at some locations, of which Irkutsk is an outstanding example. After the war the reconstruction of German enterprises followed the relocation of Soviet enterprises. Hereby, the relocation of the Buna-Werk formed the base for the city of Angarsk where one of the largest petrochemical complexes of the world is now located.

Bratsk, on the other hand, is the most famous example of Territorial Production Complexes because it is the only project, which is regarded as completed in the Soviet statistics[24]. Until the Khrushchev era, human life did not count in the economic development of Siberia. It was built upon the work of prisoners. In the 1950 the neglect of basic infrastructure like housing, food production etc. led to the realization that further development had to consider these services simultaneously with territorial production complexes. Theoretically this concept focused on the regional economy as an entity. However, as it required enormous financial resources the project started with only one TPK, the Bratsk TPK. After 1965 the structure of branch-ministries was reinstalled and the building-up of unbalanced industrial structures continued.

The industrial production of Bratsk is based on the hydro-electric power station which is an example of Soviet gigantism. Planners did not consider the demand and future consumption of this energy. Hence, at a later stage, aluminum production was located near the energy resources to create demand, and it still is one of the most important branches of the industry in the Irkutsk Oblast as can be seen from figure 2-4.

The storage lake for the hydro station has a size of 5440 km² and covers areas that once were important for the agriculture of the region. Besides the reduction in acreage, agricultural production was hampered by a scarcity of labor that was characteristic of Siberia as a whole. After forced labor was banned it became difficult to bring people to this vast unpopulated area. Though Siberia and the Irkutsk Oblast experienced enormous population growth during the Soviet pe-

23 Wein, 1999, p. 197 ff.
24 Klueter & Giese, 1990b, p. 179 ff.

riod, the number of the workforce could not keep pace with the speed of industrial development. Wandel (in Wehrheim et al., 2000) and Kurzev (1996) mention the inefficiency in the location structure of the food industry in the Siberian regions because many processing enterprises are located in urban areas rather than near to agricultural production. This is a consequence of the scarcity in the labor force and the high concentration of population in towns that lie very distant from each other. The solution planners found to allocate labor to subordinate industries was to exploit female labor in manufacturing (food processing especially) which was located in towns[25].

Figure 2-4: The Industrial Structure of the Irkutsk Oblast in 1997

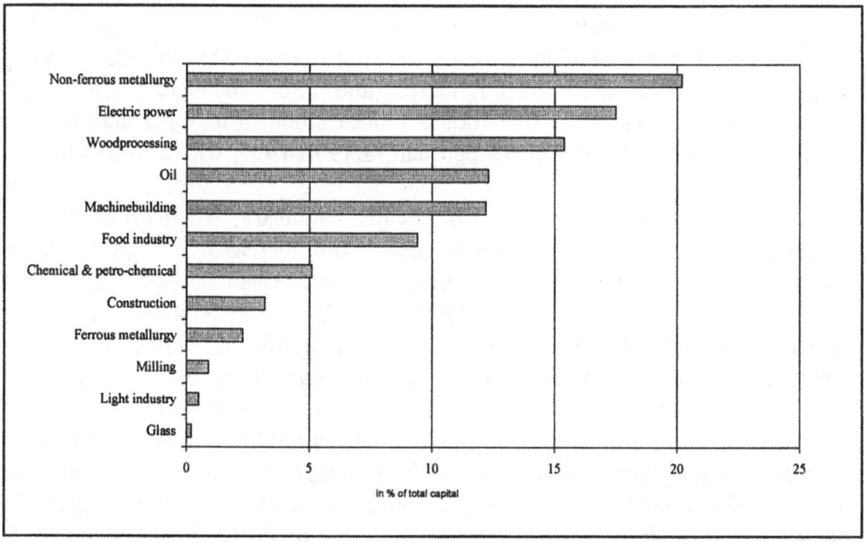

Data source: Committee for State Statistics in the Irkutsk Oblast, 1998, p. 6

For the reasons given, but also due to climatic conditions, the share of agriculture is relatively low in Eastern Siberia and the Irkutsk Oblast compared to the average level in the Russian Federation (table 2-1). The industrial structure is dominated by extractive branches (figure 2-4).

25 Shotski, 1979, pp.73-74.

Table 2-1: The Structure of the Economy in the Irkutsk Oblast, in per cent of total capital funds in1997

	Industry	Agriculture	Construction	Services
Russian Federation	36,5	12,8	4,4	46,1
Eastern Siberia	44,7	8,8	6,0	40,3
Irkutsk Oblast	42,8	7,3	7,4	42,4

Source: Goskomstat, Russian Regions, 1998, (CD-ROM)

2.4 The Impact of Transition on the Food Sector

Though the reactions to transition greatly varied over Russia's regions, the general tendency remains similar for all parts. After liberalization industrial and agricultural production in Russia fell sharply and hardly recovered. The average annual decline in industry in the Irkutsk Oblast amounts to 9 per cent between 1992-1995 and continued with 14 per cent in 1996-1997, which results in a decline of 55 per cent of the former production level. Most strongly affected are light industry, construction materials, chemical industry, wood processing and machine building while pulp and paper production increased[26]. Food processing declined by 13 per cent yearly. According to the Russian statistics, agricultural production fell to 75 per cent up to 1997 in the Russian Federation and to 78 per cent in the Irkutsk Oblast. Hence, due to a less significant decline compared to other sectors, agriculture and food processing gained in relative significance though production in absolute terms fell. However, the Irkutsk Oblast has been a net food importer for a long time, which is particularly important for bread production. Though mentioned in Wein (1999, p. 201) that the total grain production of the Oblast is used as fodder, while 100 per cent of cereals for food are imported, it will be shown that this has changed slightly during transition due to the economic situation of agricultural enterprises in transition.

The consumption side has changed by the same degree, which again showed repercussions on food production. Price increases and succeeding losses in real income had significant impact on the living conditions for Russian households. One aspect is the considerable alteration in food consumption with regard to quantity and quality. As the calorie intake in the former Soviet Union was relatively high, and overweight a widespread phenomenon, a decrease in calorie intake cannot be seen as severe. The same refers to the composition of the diet. The Soviet Union chose per capita meat consumption as an appropriate indicator to

26 Committee for State Statistics in the Irkutsk Oblast, 1998, p. 5.

prove its supposed high living standard, and according to table 2-2 could compete with the United States. Hence, the substitution of meat products by vegetable products between 1990 and 1999 can be seen as an improvement in nutrition. Notwithstanding, malnutrition was observable in the early years of transition[27].

Table 2-2: Changes in Nutrition during Transition

Per capita supply per day	USSR 1990		Russia 1999		USA 1999	
	Calories	in %	Calories	in %	Calories	in %
Total	3366	100	2879	100	3754	100
Vegetable products	2436	72	2225	77	2704	72
Animal products	931	28	654	23	1050	28
Cereals excluding beer	1254	37	1180	41	849	23

Source: FAO Food Balance Sheets USSR 1990, Russia 1999, USA 1999

Important for the present study is the significance of bread in Russian nutrition. Table 2-2 indicates cereals as a whole with a high share in total calorie intake compared to the United States. The share has increased during transition. Elsner (2000) shows that bread is an important element in the Russian diet. The share of bread in household food expenditures is 24 per cent though varying considerably over regions, and it proves to be the least elastic food item for a change in expenditure. This relatively low expenditure elasticity is confirmed by Sheng (1997) and Quaim et al. (1997) even if the coefficients tend to be less distinct in these studies.

Since most of the indicators tend to vary significantly over regions, a closer look at the developments in the Irkutsk Oblast is necessary. As mentioned above, the Irkutsk Oblast is a net importer of food and the share of food processing in the structure of the industry is relatively low compared to the Russian average. The Irkutsk Oblast has no specialization in food processing. Hence, meat is the most important branch of the food processing industry, followed by milk products and bread (figure 2-5). Meat processing and bread production are to a considerable extent based on imported raw materials.

27 Tho Seet, 1997, p. 51; p. 109 ff; Wildner, 1997.

Figure 2-5: Structure of Food Industry in the Irkutsk Oblast in 1998

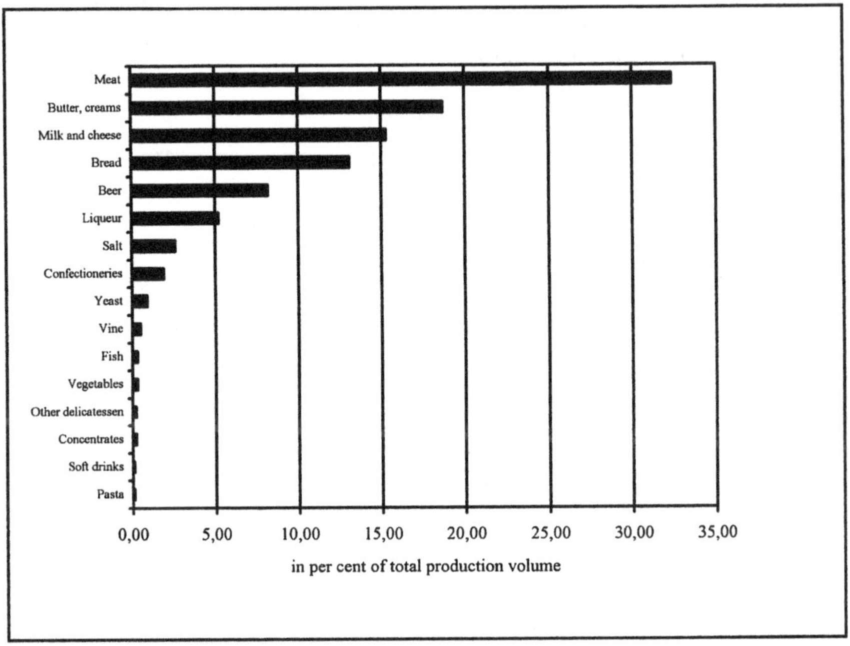

Source: Committee for State Statistics in the Irkutsk Oblast, 1999, p. 6.

Though meat appears as the most important item in the food processing industry, the picture changes significantly looking at the development of consumption and production in the Oblast. In the course of transition the decrease in meat consumption in the Irkutsk Oblast is comparable to the decline in the Russian Federation or Eastern Siberia. However, the above-mentioned substitution by vegetable products has been much stronger. While this is only a temporary phenomenon in bread, where consumption has stabilized on the same level, potato consumption remains on a much higher level than in Eastern Siberia or in the Russian Federation. The comparatively lower level of bread consumption before transition might be the first indicator of failures in the distribution system of the Soviet Union (figures 2-6 – 2-9).

The direct comparison of bread production and consumption reveals an important problem in studying transition in Russia as mentioned in the introduction. The reasons for the enormous gap between production and consumption, which even increases over the transition years, can be various. One explanation would be home production of bread. However, this would mean that the households have produced 200 000 tons of bread. Since the bread sector is very dynamic, as will be shown later, and since the share of bread in household expenditure is relatively high and the expenditure elasticity is relatively low, part of the explanation has to be assigned to statistical problems, i.e. under-reporting of production volumes and a shadow economy.

Figure 2-6: Meat Consumption in the Irkutsk Oblast during Transition

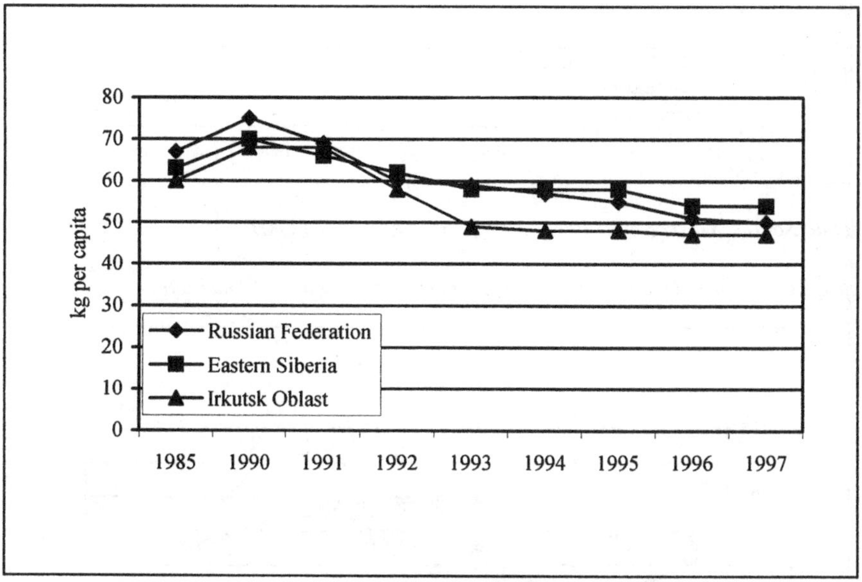

Data Source: Goskomstat, Russian Regions, 1998, (CD-ROM)

Figure 2-7: Potato Consumption in the Irkutsk Oblast during Transition

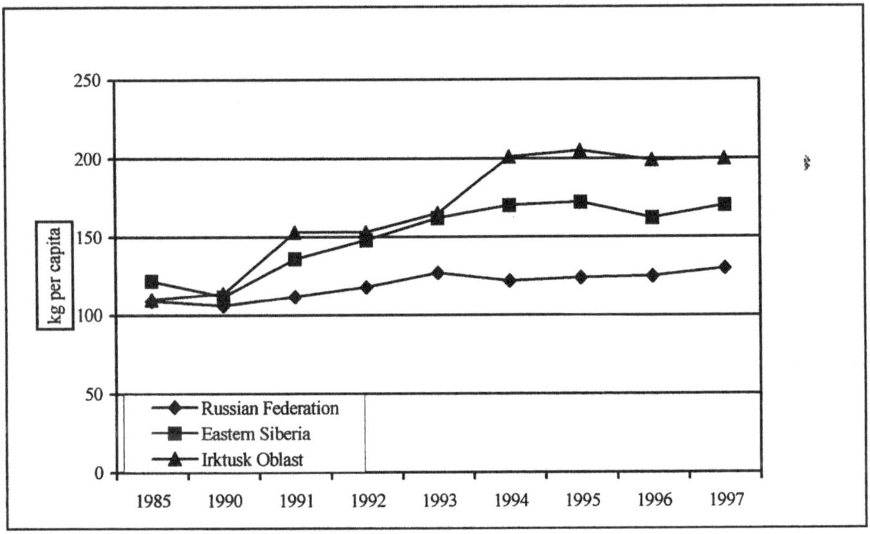

Data Source: Goskomstat, Russian Regions, 1998, (CD-ROM)

Figure 2-8: Bread Consumption in the Irkutsk Oblast during Transition

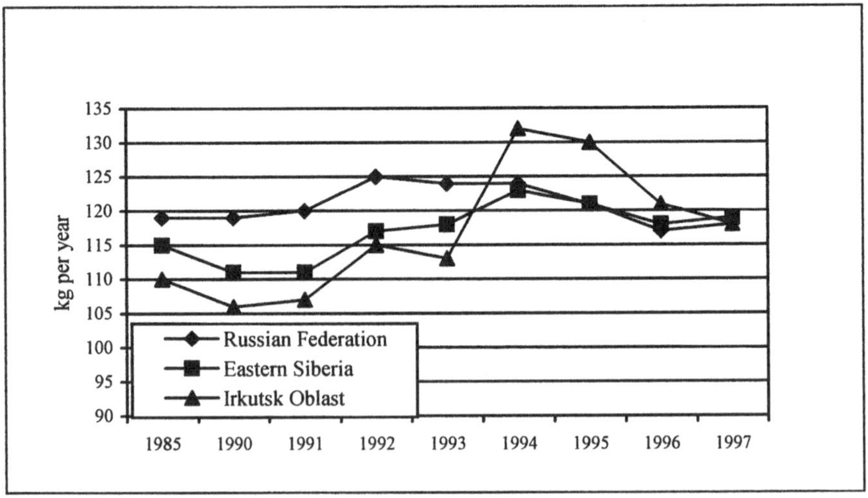

Data Source: Goskomstat, Russian Regions, 1998, (CD-ROM)

Figure 2-9: Bread Consumption and Production in the Irkutsk Oblast during Transition

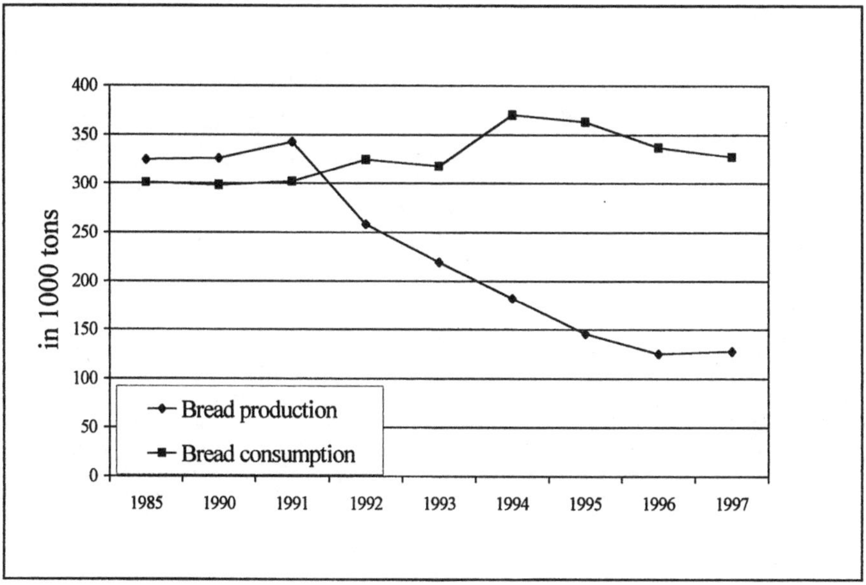

Data Source: Goskomstat, Russian Regions, 1998, (CD-ROM)

3. Spatial Allocation and the Economic System

3.1 Introduction

The production of a good can be organized in two dimensions. First, it can be distributed over production facilities ranging from only one plant to a huge number of plants. Second, these units can be distributed over space by being either concentrated in one location or dispersed. The location can furthermore be characterized by its position in relation to inputs and demand. Since one plant can be located at only one location the interrelation between the two dimensions is strong.

In the present context an industrial organization pattern is given that was shaped by a certain allocation mechanism. At some point in time the allocation mechanism was replaced because of malfunctioning that was no longer acceptable for the whole system. The distortions in the allocation results caused by imperfections in the system led to the expectation of a reallocation.

Excluding the possibility that nothing changes the first feature of production organization necessarily changes, i.e. reallocation over firms. Possible elements of this change are the growing and shrinking and the exit of existing production units as well as the entry of new units. Looking at the village-town level of spatial systems, these processes are not spatial as long as the total production at one location relative to total production at other locations does not change. In other words, while the spatial organization within a municipality (region) changes considerably, it is possible that the structure within the region (state) remains untouched.

Irrespective of the spatial level looked at, possible directions of change are dispersion and concentration. In the case of dispersion, facilities shrink that before have delivered the good to places where it is produced now. In the case of concentration, facilities emerge at one location and the good is getting delivered to locations where it was produced before. Possible changes in the second feature of spatial organization, the relative location of an element to other elements in space, are rather easy to define as moving production from demand to raw material or vice versa.

For the present study, a product was chosen that is regularly seen as not spatial, at least in European countries where the market share of fresh bread with a shelf life of 24 hours or less is relatively high compared to sliced and packed bread with a shelf life of some days[28]. In Russia sliced and packed bread has not yet emerged on the markets[29]. Hence, the transportation radius is very limited by the quality requirements of the product. But, as already mentioned in chapter one, there is nothing that is not spatial. Rather, its distribution is ubiquitous or dispersed. However, as the common trend is concentration, research regularly focuses on industries that are very much concentrated and where enterprises operate in huge domestic markets, i.e. globally or regionally. Industries, whose goods are not tradable and, consequently, operate in very small markets, gain less attention. They are regarded as dispersed although taking each market singly, they are regularly perfectly concentrated. It will become clear at a later stage that the same trend of concentration is occurring in these industries in the European countries.

As the changes in distribution and not the distribution pattern itself are of interest in the present study it is irrelevant whether the regular pattern is dispersed or concentrated. The basic task is to understand whether the change takes the 'right' or the 'wrong' direction. That is not easy to judge as rights and wrongs always require a reference system. The basic criterion in economic analysis should be the efficiency gains achieved by the reallocation. The theoretical deductions in this chapter give insights into how an efficient pattern would look and where new inefficiencies can be expected.

The aim of this chapter is to draw hypotheses on the direction of changes explained above in the allocation of bread production between plants and locations. Therefore, the first part illustrates the planned economy allocation process, shows the theoretical results of allocation in a sample region and describes the malfunctioning that appeared. The second part is devoted to the nature of market economy allocation and derives the result of spatial allocation for the same regional situation as in the planned economy scenario. As the specificities of the transition economy might have a significant influence on the reallocation, section three gives an overview and summarizes the possible directions of impact. Finally, the conclusion integrates the starting pattern, the expected market economy result and the possible transition-specific distortions into hypotheses on the actual development and the significance of the respective factors.

28 Sutton, 1991, pp. 403-411; www.baeko.de/Inhalte/Service/brotmarkt.htm.

29 The hygienic conditions in Russian food retail are under discussion. Traditionally bread is handed out without any packaging and it is left to the consumer to bring it home in a clean manner. Kommersant, 29.05.2000.

3.2 The Planned Economy Distribution Process and Resulting Pattern in Bread Production

3.2.1 The Planner's Task

The economies of socialist and communist countries can be characterized by the degree to which market activity is allowed. While some countries like Hungary allowed markets with a view to price signals for a more efficient allocation, the economy of the Soviet Union can be regarded as an almost perfect command economy[30].

Theoretically, the basis of a planned economy is that the political leadership and planning organs claim to know the needs of the society, i.e. of each enterprise and of each individual. Accordingly, the center has to allocate each single good in the necessary amount to producers and consumers, i.e. housing, clothing, furniture, food etc. to the households and machines, raw materials, workers and other inputs to the plants. As resources are scarce, the planner has to allocate efficiently with a view to the society's welfare. For this purpose he has to know consumer preferences and the efficiency of alternative production technologies. Since the center, and only the center, has all the information it has to communicate to all actors in the economy when and where they have to produce what, and how much of it and where they have to deliver production. Because enterprises do not get information about quantities and qualities directly from their customers, be it other enterprises or the final consumer, they theoretically have to be given commands as precise as that in March and April they have to produce x pairs of black working shoes size 48 design 'Siberia'. Hence, in January and February enterprise Y has to produce a corresponding number of black bootlaces and enterprise A leather etc. Consequently, planners have to harmonize production along all existing production chains for all enterprises.

The complexity of the planner's task requires channeling the decision-making. In the command economy of the Soviet Union branch ministries formulated sectoral plans[31] while regional plans[32] were proposed by the committee of

30 The following explanations on the planned economy are based on the standard literature by Nove, 1977 and Kornai 1995. All more detailed information is based on interviews with planners at SOPS as well as the reading of basic planning materials in the same institute. Furthermore: Council for the study of production forces 1971, 1972, 1984, 1989, 1992.

31 Skhemy rasvitiya i rasmeshtsheniya otrasley narodnogo khosyaistva i otrasli promyshlennosti.

32 Skhemy rasvitiya i rasmeshtsheniya proisvoditelnykh sil po ekonomicheskim paionam i soysnym respublikam.

union-republic ministries. As the regional plans contain information on sectors, and sectoral plans contain information on regional distribution, and each ministry and committee represents different positions, the various interests had to be harmonized to guarantee economic development. This was done in a general plan[33] which brought together regional and sectoral propositions. This planning can be regarded as long-term investment planning as the plans had to be in compliance with the five-year plans and long-term political planning and thus correspond to their time horizon. On this level of republics and regions the plans have a balanced character. For each time period they present data on the existing capacities, on the expected demand and on the necessary investments derived from this information. The planners used input-output coefficients to fix production targets and to reach these by input control.

For consumer good industries and, in particular, the food industry the rule of regional autarky prevailed. The goal was that each region produced sufficient food to provide for its population, and that was the basic assumption of investment planning. Hence, as in this understanding regional food imports have a temporary character, they did not play a role in decision-making. Thus the calculations for medium- and long-term investment planning in the food industry were as follows: the planner calculates the future demand for a certain product in each region using trends in population developments, recommendations on calorie intake and the composition of the diet. In these calculations regional and ethnic differences are taken into account. For example, in the northern resource exploiting region with sharp climatic conditions a higher calorie intake is assumed, because of a higher proportion of male persons employed in physically exhausting work. The necessity for capacities over different time-scales (five to fifteen years) are calculated and compared to existing capacities. So far, the plans provide information about average numbers but at the next step the planning has to become more detailed. If a lack in capacities can be expected, the planner considers various means, like reconstruction, modernization, extension and new construction. The plans contain information about all enterprises in the region and their physical state. Where possible the planner opts for the former three means in order to save capital. To some extent these are also location decisions as the planner has to decide which location to extend or modernize. However, these decisions are mainly guided by considerations of technical feasibility. But when it comes to deciding on new projects by which the previously calculated requirements shall be fulfilled, the planner has to decide on the size and number of production units and their specific location.

33 Generalnaya skhema rasmeshtsheniya proisvoditelnykh sil SSSR.

3.2.2 The Planners' Solution

To find the optimal industry structure, i.e. size and location of plants, the planner was provided with so-called technical-economic indicators by the scientific institutes at Gosplan. The indicators basically consider production and transportation where the basic task can be described as to optimise the interplay between production costs and transportation costs with the goal to minimize total resource employment as illustrated in figure 3-1.

As the products in the food industry are manifold and show different characteristics, it is necessary to analyse each good individually. While the technical-economic indicators for most of the products assumed that production is cheaper in larger plants due to lower employment of capital stocks per unit, the products reveal stark differentiation in transportation. The characteristics of the product affect transportability and transportation costs. Relevant characteristics include not only the final product itself but also the inputs used in the production process.

Figure 3-1: Determination of Plant Sizes by Average Costs

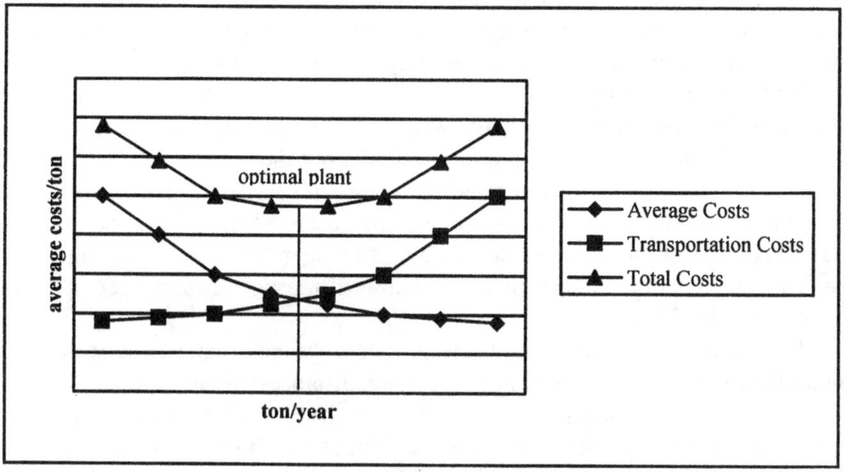

Source: author's own figure

The basic inputs of all food items are agricultural raw materials, which may be processed in only one step or in a number of steps. In the case of milk, for example, the marketing chain could be either limited to packaging and marketing to the final consumer, or it could be extended by another step like processing milk into butter or cheese. Other products like confectionery require a range of already processed agricultural products (sugar, flour, cacao etc.). Thus, the position where the respective product stands in the production chain plays another important role. In contrast to other industrial products, food items are perishable which can considerably limit their transportability. This is not linked to their position in the production chain. It is possible that the raw material is more perishable than the processed good, for example milk compared to butter: at the same time it is possible that the processed good is more perishable than the inputs, as in the case of confectionery or bread. According to the differences in product characteristics, factors determining the spatial system are of very different significance in each product.

Density of raw materials and transportation costs: At the beginning of the chain stands the collection of the agricultural raw material and its transportation to the first processing stage. The basic technical-economic indicators for this step were the density of the raw material on the one hand and the perishability of the product and transportation infrastructure on the other hand as these factors determine the transportation radius around a processing facility. The idea was to assign a raw material zone to each processing plant whereby the density and the perishability determine the number and size of the entities. The lower the raw material density the more transportation occurs to put a certain capacities to work, or the lower the raw material density the more, and smaller, processing facilities had to be installed.

Economies of scale and transportation costs: This posed considerable problems to the planners: according to their calculations there were always economies of scale in most of the industries and the saving of capital was their overall goal. The minimum plant size was too large to be sustained by the low raw material densities. Neither were the technical state of refrigeration and packaging nor the road surface conditions such that they allowed transport distances compared to other countries.

Weight loss materials: For some products the raw material as well as the processed output can be transported further distances (living animals – frozen meat, grain – flour, sugar beet – sugar). For these products another technical-economic indicator applied, which is the famous weight-loss rule coined by Alfred Weber (1909). After processing, the weight of output could be either equal to the weight of inputs, or higher or lower. In the case that the unit of output is heavier than the unit of input, production is located at the point of consumption: in the case that the unit of output is lighter than the unit of input, production is located at the point of collection. Nevertheless, the concept of raw material zones still applies.

Density of demand and transportation costs: Furthermore, there are food items which are produced at the location of consumption though not due to the weight loss rule. They are located next to consumption because the final product is perishable but the inputs are not. In these cases the number and size of facilities is determined by the density of demand and the transportation radius allowed by the transportation infrastructure and the perishability of the product. According to the raw materials zones, each producer of final products was assigned to a demand zone.

3.2.3 Location Structure of the Bread Industry

The industry which is of interest in the present study, i.e. bread production, clearly belongs to the products described in the last paragraph. Bread baking facilities are located near to consumption. Though the final product is heavier than the raw materials this is not due to transportation costs but due to the physical characteristics. While the main input flour can be stored, Russian bread cannot be stored and is usually consumed within the same day. Furthermore, to cover the whole range of bread products the organization had to be such that retail outlets could be supplied several times a day. According to the planning guidelines this reduced the possible transportation radius to 30-50 km in 1970. In contrast to other products, like meat, there is no hint that the supply of raw material influenced the calculations. Hence, the remaining variable is the size of the plant, which again depends on the population and the estimated consumption that lay at 100 kg bread per capita per year in 1970. Moreover, as in other products so in bread production, economies of scale were assumed. The average costs of one ton of bread in a facility with a capacity of 30 t per 24h was calculated 7-9% higher than in a facility with a capacity of 130t per 24h. However, even the smallest calculated projects (table 3-1) are too large for settlements in rural areas and the establishment of smaller entities is inevitable. But as this is not efficient the recommendation was to build one large entity and deliver even further than the assumed radius.

Table 3-1: Project Sizes for Bread Plants in the Soviet Union in 1970

Capacity, t/24h	Production per year in 1000 tons	Number of population provided in 1000
30	10,5	100
45	15,9	150
65	21,8	200
130	44,7	500

Source: SOPS, 1971, p. 262.

The rules for the planner can be summarized as follows:

- Bread has to be produced at the settlements.
- The largest possible facilities are to be realized. The typical projects are as shown in table 3-1.
- Where inevitable, plants of a smaller size (6-12 tons/24h) had to be realized.
- Bread should not be transported further than 50 km.
- In the case of low density of demand bread can be transported further than 50 km.
- There are no calculations on transportation costs.

Figure 3-2 shows a region with settlements of three different sizes. Three large settlements lie along a main communication route while small and medium-sized settlements are peripheral to the large settlements. However, the medium sized settlements south of the main communication line are well connected to the large settlements while only the medium sized settlement in the north is connected to one large settlement. The distances between the large and medium-sized settlements in the south are less than the distance between medium and large settlements in the north.

The task of the planner is to satisfy all the demands for bread in the region. The settlements have the sizes 1', 50' and 200' respectively as indicated by the scale of the signs.

To summarize, the above rules state that costs are minimized with maximum size of production facilities, with transportation neglected in the calculation of total costs. Table 3-1 shows typical projects for bread plants for settlements of the size 100', 150', 200' and 500'. As the three large settlements (population 200') fit into a typical project, the decision for these entities is clear. In each city a plant of the size 45t/24h is located that serves the local market.

The size of all other settlements lies below the level of the minimum typical project for a settlement of 100'. The distances between small settlements and medium and large settlements south of the main communication line lie within the radius of 50 km. A settlement size of 50' justifies according to the ratios in Table 3-1 a production facility of 15 tons/24h which is still above the very small entities of 6 to 12 tons/24h. It follows that in each settlement of 50' in the southern area a bread facility is established. The capacity necessary to serve the population of a settlement of size 1 is 0,3 tons/24h. This is below the given level of 6 tons for a very small unit. Hence, the small settlements will be served with bread by the nearest larger unit, i.e. from the large or medium settlements. For the settlements in the northern areas, it follows that one facility is established in the medium settlement. The distances between the small settlements exceed the 50 km.

However, as it is costly to build smaller facilities, bread is transported to these settlements too and the population has to accept losses in quality.

Figure 3-2: Spatial Organization of the Bread Industry in a Planned Economy

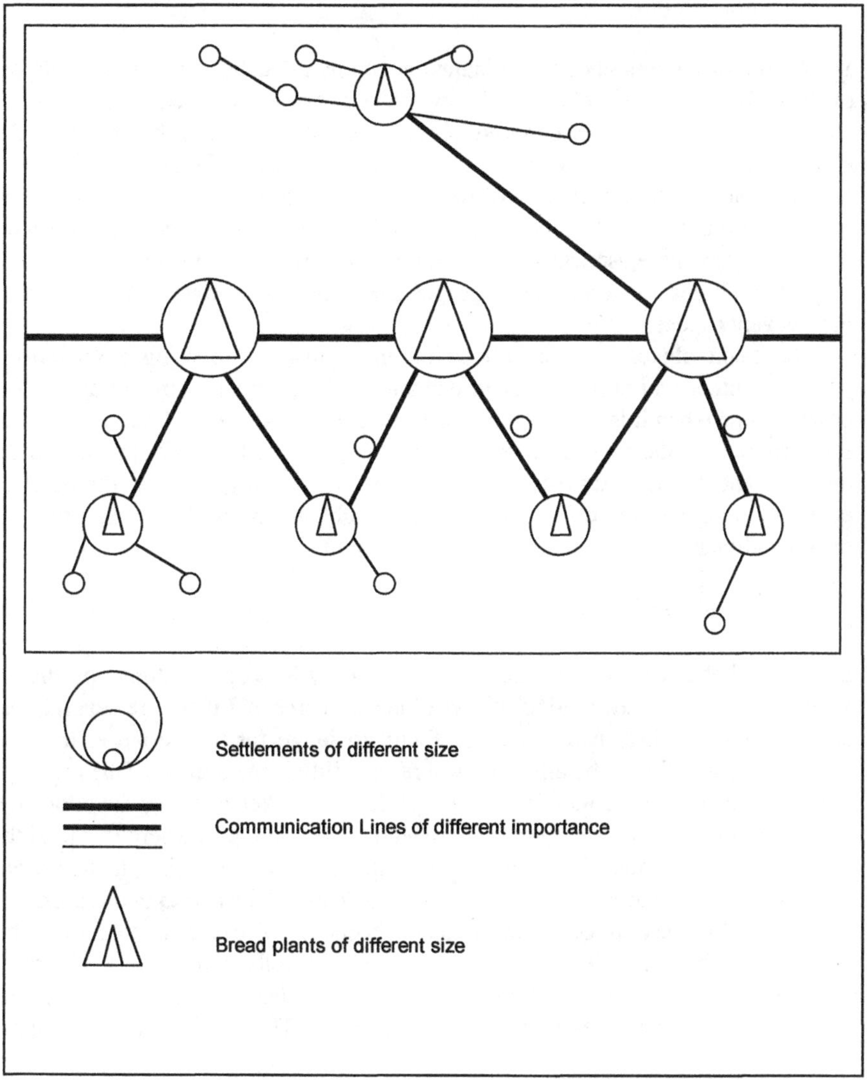

Source: author's own drawing

At the end, eight bread baking facilities are active in the region and all settlements are served with bread.

3.2.4 Malfunctioning

So far, the discussion about the planned economy allocation process was almost exclusively theoretical. While in theory the result of each allocation mechanism led to efficiency, in reality either system showed imperfections that led to inefficiencies. However, as the world had witnessed in the case of planned economies, inefficiencies led to a total break-down of the whole system. Only the description of the enormous task of planners might suffice to explain the failure. However, there are many more aspects in the system that contributed to the decline. Though they are well-described and documented[34], it seems appropriate to briefly repeat the relevant aspects.

The main objective of an allocation mechanism is to bring a good to a place/consumer where it is most in demand in the particular amount and at the point in time when it is demanded. This sentence presents several dimensions that serve to explain the failures in the system: the utility of the good, the spatial dimension and the time dimension. While the utility of a good is at the heart of economic thinking, the other two represent problems in the distribution process once the dimensions of the good are decided upon.

Utility, Scarcity and Prices

Economic behaviour sets in when there is scarcity in a certain thing and the respective thing becomes a good. If something is scarce and there are several possible usages, a criterion needs to be found to judge for the best use. In other words, the good should be allocated where its utility is maximized. This principle is independent of the economic system. While in a market economy the allocation process in this respect is easy to comprehend – the good goes where it is paid the highest price, the idea of scarcity is rather difficult to find in the planned economy distribution process and decision-making. This can be due to two reasons.

Firstly, the description of the planned economy distribution process so far showed that there is little scope to take utility or scarcity into account. The planner started from a certain need and calculated capacities accordingly, i.e. the goal was to reach a balance between supply and demand. The quantity at which supply

34 Nove, 1977; Kornai, 1995; Degras & Nove, 1964; Nove &Zauberman, 1964; Wiles, 1964; Rumer, 1984; Schroeder, 1989.

and demand are balanced was determined by the demand the planner calculated. Hence, there was no mechanism that automatically adjusted the quantity towards other goods, and subsequently investments, like the price mechanism does in a market economy. If, for example, the price reaches a certain level a consumer will choose not to consume the respective good but to allocate his/her income to another good; or a producer at a certain level of interest rate would choose to allocate his capital to other uses where the rent is higher. This shows the very basic difference between the two systems and the problematic nature of a definition of need. The planned economy uses an absolute concept of need: as much as you want, and it assumes to know the quantities wanted. Furthermore, it assumes these quantities to be fixed over relatively long periods of time as the description of investment planning has shown. Consequently, by this assumption, the budget constraints economic actors face in market economics are abolished and the law of scarcity is repealed.

Moreover, the action of the planners was not consistent. If the planner knew all needed quantities in all products, it logically follows that knowledge of money and prices were not necessary and the planner simply needed to mete out the respective shares to each consumer and producer. But, to ease the vertical links, planners had to introduce a unit to make comparable the calculation of goods that are measured in different dimensions. These units were electricity or a monetary unit. Furthermore, there was a need to organize final consumption by the consumer. Thus, workers received money wages and bought consumer goods for regulated prices. Though these prices were fixed and calculated on a cost-plus basis, they still functioned as signals to the consumer.

Bread is a very famous example for this process. As a most basic food item it was assigned extremely low prices, which led to increasing demand. Consumers started to use bread for other purposes, like for example fodder for animals. Given that there was then much more demand for bread than planners had calculated, and adding the spatial dimension, the result was as planners themselves perceived and stated in their writings: There was underprovision of bread in rural areas and, as a consequence, the share of home-baked bread was high. There is no proof, but it is easy to imagine that bread was first distributed where it was produced and if the production was not sufficient a deficit emerged in more distant regions.

Supply Chain Management

Not only did the fixed assumptions regarding consumption lead to distortions in the results of the planned economy distribution process, but also the vertical relations between enterprises were at least theoretically fixed, as has been shown in the preceding sections, i.e. producers could not choose their suppliers. However, it is always possible that disturbances in the production process occur because of technical problems or accidents. But a delay in production has consequences for all production steps down the chain because a lack in necessary inputs emerges. The fixed system of supply chains showed little redundancy that would have allowed enterprises to react to such a situation. Enterprises developed strategies to cope with such situations by bartering with other enterprises or in starting to produce their own inputs. The problem of integrating the supply chain became particularly severe in the agro- food sector. As a result, the concept of agro-industrial-complexes was designed with the purpose of integrating all steps in agricultural production and its processing into one complex. However, only limited improvements were reached[35].

Overestimation of Economies of Scale and Capital

Crucial for the configuration of industry and hence the location structure are the assumptions on returns to scale. As mentioned above, planners assumed economies of scale in almost all products and as a result opted for rather big production units. At a later point in the discussion of the bread market, it will be shown that the industry configuration of the German bread market does not give a hint that existing economies of scale in the production of bread though tendencies of concentration can be observed.

In the particular case of bread, calculations by the planners are available from which they concluded that economies of scale exist in most of the inputs involved. However, the author could not find a plausible economic reason for the assumption of economies of scale in bread production, and therefore concludes that the planners were mistaken in this respect. As bread does not belong to the list of products the production of which was very much influenced by political and ideological reasoning, this argument does not serve as a reason either. One possibility is the tendency to overestimate the value of capital. As a result planners tended to save capital where possible and even tended to maintain enterprises whose capital and technology were almost exhausted. As a result there was little scope to adjust the industry structure towards more efficient configurations.

35 Kurzev, 1995, pp. 140-154; Stadelbauer, 1996, pp. 469-471; Romanov, 1998, pp.68-73; Vashtshanov, et al., 1995, pp. 65-74; Wandel, 2001, pp. 32-42; for detailed overviews over several sectors see contributions in Hartmann & Wandel, 2001.

Institutional aspects

As in any other society so also in a communist country there are phenomena that can be described with the terminology of institutional economics like principal-agent problem or moral hazard. This complex impacts in two ways. Investment decisions in general are based on ideological or political decisions but are also guided by the interests of institutions or individuals. In the process of sectoral and regional planning that was described in section 3.2.1 there was much scope for powerful ministries and ambitious individuals to influence decision-making processes towards their own interests.

Secondly, the planner was not able to collect all information by himself, but rather he had to rely on data that was reported by enterprise directors and regional authorities. The management of enterprises benefited from reporting plan-fulfilment or overfulfilment. Hence, there was a strong incentive for managers to report figures that were in compliance with expectations. However, as the assumption of the whole system is that the planner has all the information, the false information the planner was provided with led inevitably to inefficient investment and production decisions.

3.3 Market Mechanism

3.3.1 Decision-Making in a Market Economy in Contrast to a Planned Economy

Profit-Maximization

In the case of the market economy the discussion starts with two elements that are different to the planned economy case, firstly the perspective of the decision-maker, secondly the target variable. While in the planned economy case the planner decided with the target to minimize the costs or the employment of the society's resources, in the market economy the decision-making shifts to an entrepreneur with the target to maximize his own profits. If the industry is a perfect monopoly, the decision-maker decides over the whole industry and is, to some extent, comparable to the planner. If there is more than one entrepreneur in the industry there is also more than one decision-maker.

How decisions in an enterprise are made and which goals are pursued depends very much on the organization itself. As enterprises in mature market economies have turned into huge organizational entities where decision-making is transferred from the enterprise owners to salaried management, the assumption of profit maximization has been questioned[36]. However, the present study deals with businesses in a very simple industry that start from scratch where unity between management and ownership is given and profit maximization is plausible[37].

Ownership and Location Structure

However, there is another aspect in ownership that should be mentioned in the context of location structure. That is the possible difference between ownership and production structure. If each production facility represents an enterprise, production structure and ownership are identical. It is possible though that ownership and production structure are not identical if one enterprise maintains more than one production location. This has an impact on the concentration of the industry as a whole which is much higher in this case than in the case where all facilities are operated under separate responsibility. It has no impact on the location structure. Rather, economic reasons force the owner to operate several production facilities, and spatial dispersion remains under concentrated ownership.

Open Economy and Location Structure

As in a planned economy, production and transportation costs are the determining factors in a market economy and, again, the peculiarities of the product determine the location near either raw material or demand. However, the geographical scope changes considerably. Planners did not consider imports of raw materials in their location decisions, though imports and inter-regional trade within the Soviet Union were significant. In a market economy entrepreneurs have to decide on their supplies themselves, and in certain products (like grain) face a global market, while for other products with low transportability the extent of their factor markets is regional or local. The target in the procurement is to minimize the total input costs, that is the purchasing price plus transportation costs. Given that agricultural production costs differ around the globe, extremely low production costs in a distant region can offset the relatively high transportation costs and a clear rule for this relation between transportation costs and location is difficult to find[38].

---

36 Furubotn, 2000.
37 Lim & Shumway, 1992.
38 Lundgren, 1996 for the development of separate markets due to changes in transportation.

3.3.2 Spatial Allocation of the Bread Industry under the Conditions of a Market Economy

Though some crucial prerequisites change in a market economy setting compared to a planned economy setting the transportability of the good remains a crucial factor. At the first stage of the food production chain, i.e. the collection and processing of agricultural raw materials, again the peculiarities of the raw material determine. Where the raw material is perishable, processing is going to be located near to the location of agricultural production. Where either the raw material or the processed good can be transported, the offsetting of production and transportation costs and the weight-loss-rule explained above can be applied. However, the weight-loss rule applies only for a few products, for instance sugar beet. In many products technology is advanced enough to permit products to be transported over long distances. If the final product is perishable and the input is not, the rule of offsetting production costs against transportation costs applies for the procurement but the production is located near to the consumer.

As in a planned economy, bread belongs to the latter products. Hence, the location choice is independent of the input and production is located where demand is. This characteristic of the product at the same time determines the size of the market which is given by the quality requirements and the transportability of the product. Hence, the size of the market is the reachable demand which is the demand at the location where the facility is located plus the demand within a radius in which the production can be transported without a loss in quality. Given the same region as in the planned economy example, only this factor will lead to a huge number of markets.

Total coverage is given if all settlements, thus the total population, are part of a geographical market. Population that is located more distant from a bakery than the perishability of the product allows is not covered by a geographical market. This is due to the economic law that the demand that is reachable from the respective production location warrants viability for an enterprise, i.e. covers the sunk set-up costs and the minimum fixed costs[39]. Below this level an enterprise would make losses and cannot survive. There is a variety of settlement configurations that would warrant this minimum size for viability in the respective radius. The minimum size could be reached by the population in one settlement, in two settlements or in several very small settlements.

However, above the minimum level of market size the determination of market structure becomes the crucial question. The determinants of market structure are a broad issue in industrial economics regarding industries with huge domestic

39 Asplund, 1998, p. 2

markets in mature market economies, for example when it comes to the determinants of monopolies and oligopolies and different strategic behaviour. However, in a simple industry like the bread industry that starts from scratch, the most simple assumptions suffice to explain market structure[40], i.e. market size and economies of scale.

It was mentioned before that planners assumed economies of scale in bread production, and hence limited the size of enterprises downwards. Furthermore, it was stated that there is no plausible reason to assume economies of scale in bread production. A description of the German bread market is believed to give some evidence.

Excursus: The German Bread Market *The German bread market serves as an appropriate example for comparison as the consumer habits in bread consumption are similar to the Russian habits. Though the per capita consumption is much less than in Russia, it is the highest in the European Union with 84 kg per year*[41]*. As in Russia, bread in Germany is traditionally consumed freshly and has to be sold on the day of production. Other forms of bread like sliced and packed bread or frozen bread products exist. While sliced and packed bread is usually sold in supermarkets and produced by bread factories, the traditional bread producer and provider of fresh bread is the local bakery, which formed an entity in production and retailing. Though these bakeries still exist and still hold a considerable market share, the bread market has experienced a concentration process which has started in large markets. Sutton (1992, p. 405) estimates the share of traditional bakeries up to 70 per cent in 1985, while in 2000 the share of bread sold through bakeries is estimated at 54.5 per cent*[42]*. With this process the unity of production and retailing has vanished. Bakeries started to bake bread centrally and maintain retail facilities throughout the town. So far the process has not led to complete monopolies in large towns. Usually a smaller number of bakeries with a varying number of retail facilities and a larger number of bakeries which unite production and retailing coexist. For instance, the yellow pages (2001) of the city of Bonn reports the following structure as shown in table 3-2.*

Later in the process even national brands in bread production have developed. In 1998 Kamps went public and became the leading bread producer in Germany by buying small bakeries as well as industrial producers all over Europe. However, in Germany Kamps has become a brand that is well known

40 Asplund, 1998; Sutton, 1991.
41 www.laugenbrezel.com/page.php.p-wissenswertes.
42 www.baeko.de/Inhalte/service/brotmarkt.htm.

and that uses advertising to increase its market shares. While this is an enormous concentration process in ownership, spatial concentration has occurred through advances in technology but is still limited by the quality requirements: Kamps operates 23 large-scale bakeries in Germany that supply retail outlets with bread and intermediate products that are baked in the stores[43]*. Though concentration is high compared to the fragmented traditional markets, production within the company is dispersed due to the peculiarities of the industry and requires a sophisticated logistic system.*

Table 3-2: Production Structure of the Bread Industry, City of Bonn in 2001.

Number of retail facilities per enterprise	Number of enterprises	Percentage of facilities
30	1	16.95
19	1	10.73
9	1	5.08
7	1	3.95
6	1	3.39
5	2	5.65
4	2	4.52
3	6	10.17
2	9	10.17
1	52	29.38

Source: Yellow Pages, City of Bonn, 2001

Given the fact that bread-making is a very old industry, and that concentration processes have started relatively late in a mature market economy like Germany, the assumption of economies of scale for the Russian situation does not seem plausible. The concentration in the German market is a consequence of changes in technology, for example the use of frozen dough[44], which leads actually to a segmented market, and in marketing and distribution. Economies of scale that explain this development cannot be regarded as relevant for the Russian market where entrepreneurship just has started to develop. In the following discussion, average costs are assumed to behave as shown in figure 3-3. At the beginning of the curve the minimum size of viability (y^M) is not reached, and as long as the average cost curve has not reached this point no enterprise opens. Where average costs reach viability they remain stable over a variety of possible sizes but at a certain size they start to increase again. Above this level more than one firm will necessarily emerge. Where the market size is between once and twice the mini-

43 Kamps Annual Report 2000, p. 22.
44 Sutton, 1991, p. 405.

mum size only one enterprise can survive: where this size is exceeded, two enterprises can survive but so also can one larger enterprise.

Figure 3-3: Assumed average cost curve for the bread industry

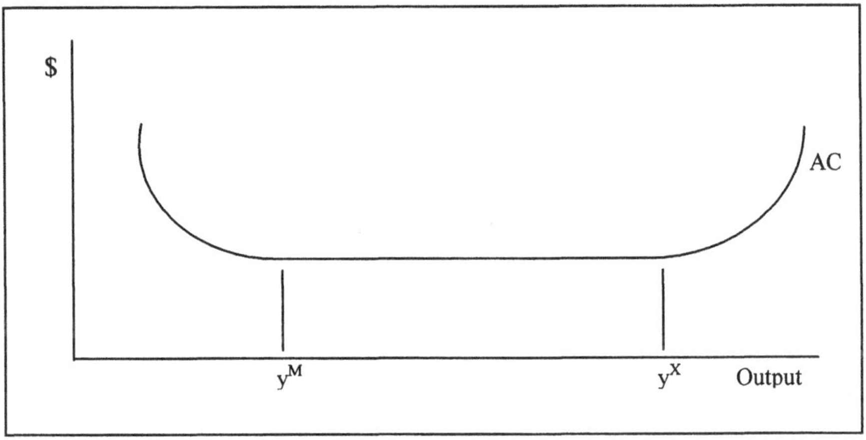

Source: Panzar in Schmalensee, 1989, p. 37

Within the same geographical market the market size can differ considerably according to the population living within its radius. Hence, the reachable demand could be less than the minimum scale to warrant viability, more than this scale, or more than the maximum efficient scale. As a result, in a geographical market where demand is less than the minimum scale, demand remains unmet; in geographical markets where demand is between this minimum and maximum efficient scale, a single producer can serve the total demand, and where the maximum efficient scale is exceeded, more than one producer can serve the market.

3.3.3 Location Structure of the Bread Industry in a Market Economy

Now give the same region for an example as in the preceding paragraph: however, the economic system is a free market economy. So far there is no baker in the region to meet the demand. Given that a single entrepreneur enters the region and decides to open a bakery, he has a free choice of location. The decision rule for the entrepreneur is to maximize the expected profits at the specific location. The profit depends on the price taken for the production sold and the costs of the production. To simplify the discussion, costs are assumed not to differ between the locations. As he at this stage represents the only baker in the region, he can choose the price and the quantity as well. However, the entrepreneur faces constraints. As an individual at the start of a business-undertaking, available financial resources restrict the size of the production facility. Furthermore, he has to expect that others will follow his example as the production he is able to provide at the beginning is limited and demand will remain unmet. Hence, he has to consider the future perspective of profit. Given low barriers to entry and low sunk costs the bread market can be expected to be a contestable market where a monopolist cannot exhaust his monopoly rent because he has to fear the entry of a competitor who accepts lower prices. Consequently, the first entrepreneur could choose any location[45]. Here the first entrepreneur prefers a future monopoly position because he assumes that the entrepreneurs who will follow will go to large markets first as long as the demand in these markets is not fully satisfied, and shy away from possible price battles in a monopoly market. Subsequently, he expects to realize at least a small monopoly rent at the beginning of his operations.

The small settlements in the region do not guarantee the viability of the production. Therefore, they are not an alternative. Yet the medium and large settlements do. The size of the small settlements is between minimum scale and twice the minimum scale. Hence, they are suitable for a monopoly position. The entrepreneur can afford to install a facility large enough to serve the whole settlement. As there are five settlements of this size, he has to consider where to settle. Given that he faces the same demand curve in each of these settlements he considers the cost situation. Production costs are the same at each location. The procurement of inputs is dependent on the location. Wholesale flour is located in the large settlements only. The wholesale prices are the same at each large settlement. As transportation of inputs would incur higher costs to the settlement in the north, the entrepreneur excludes this possibility. To choose the right location out of the remaining four, the entrepreneur considers another aspect. Small settlements where bakeries are not going to appear are connected to the medium settlements. Nevertheless, there is a demand for bread in these settlements. The distances between these settlements are such that transportation of production would still guarantee quality of the product and, though transportation increases the price, demand at this price would still bring profit. Hence, he decides to locate at the settlement in the west and also to serve the three settlements connected to it.

Other bakers follow the example and in time all markets are captured. In the settlements south of the main communication line all settlements are served with bread. In the northern area only the medium settlement is provided with bread as distances to the small settlements are too large to make transportation feasible

45 Fritsch et al., 1999, pp. 201-212.

and profitable. In the three large settlements competitive markets have developed as all entrepreneurs in the beginning face the same financial constraint and are not able to meet the whole demand in the settlement and therefore have to share. As the settlements are four times larger than the minimum scale, four bakeries can be found in these markets. Hence, 17 bread baking facilities can be found in the region where five small settlements are not provided with bread.

However, there are differences in profits and prices. Again it is assumed that bakers in a monopoly position can realize at least a minimum monopoly rent. The northern baker has to charge the highest price due to a higher cost situation which decreases his profits compared to the bakers in the southern area. Bakers in the competitive market face marginal cost pricing, and hence lower profits, than the monopoly bakeries. Consequently, the highest price is in the north, a lower price in the south and the lowest price along the main communication line.

3.4 Discussion of the Results

The comparison of the organization of bread production in the planned economy case and the market economy case shows that there are similarities as well as differences.

Dispersed industry: In either system the industry has to be characterized as dispersed. This is not surprising as the specificity of the product remains and imposes certain limitations on spatial concentration. However, the results depend on the assumptions made. The scale of the settlements chosen has a strong tendency to large settlements, which stems from the original figures obtained from the planner's literature. However, there is a huge range of possible settlement sizes between 1' and 50'. While the example sizes are sufficient to explain the planned case in the given range, there is much more to happen in a market economy.

The industry in reality can be expected to be much more dispersed. However, the rule of monopolies in small markets, oligopolies in medium- sized markets and competitive markets in large areas persists. As a result, firm sizes in the market economy case are significantly smaller and the number of plants is higher than in the planned economy case.

It was stated that the present argument sees the assumption of economies of scale in the planned scenario as a simple mistake. What would change in the planned economy scenario under the assumption of no economies of scale? Nothing would change in the large settlements as long as the firm size does not exceed the maximum efficient scale. There is no plausible reason for a planner to operate more than one unit in one settlement. However, the assumption of economies of scale had an impact on the provision of small settlements with bread. As shown,

Figure 3-4: Spatial Organization of the Bread Industry in a Market Economy

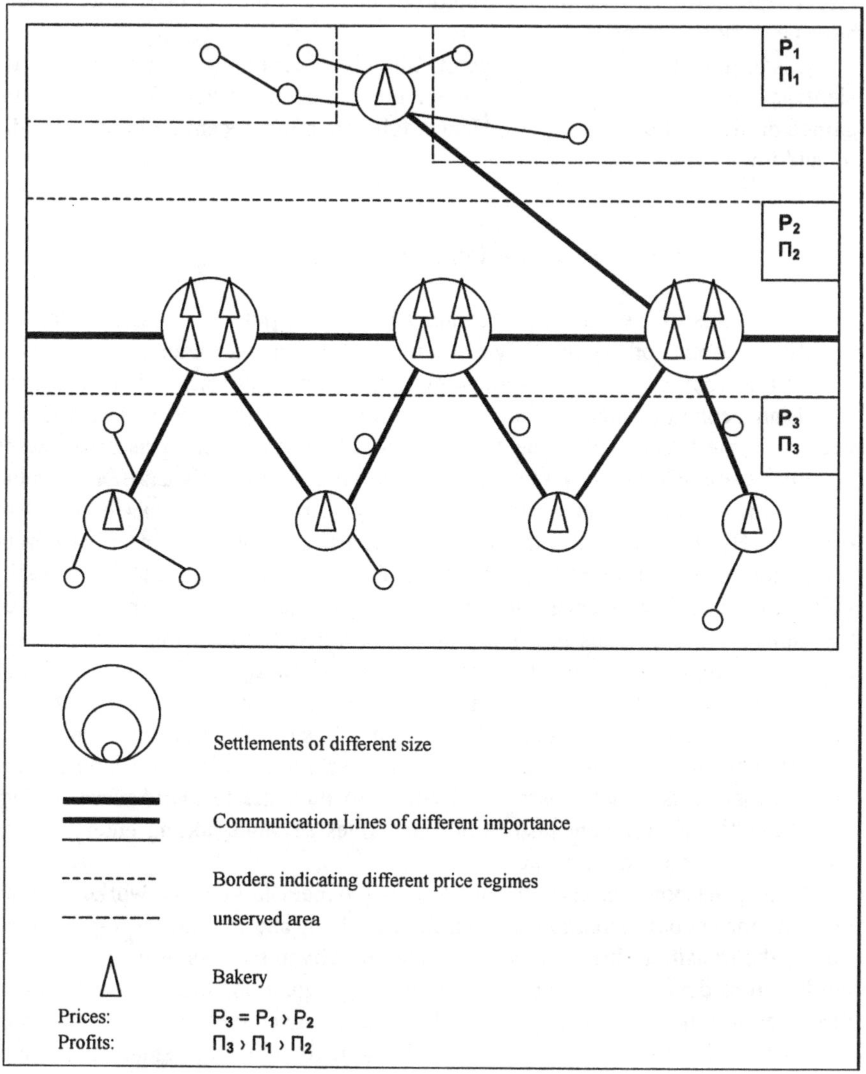

Source: author's own drawing

bread production is viable at much lower capacities than planners assumed. Hence, the downward limitation would not have existed and production would have been more dispersed.

This argument confirms that theoretically either economic system can be efficient as the determining factors remain the same, and that efficiency can be gained at different configurations. Hence, failures in the system lie in the feasibility and implementation.

3.5 Spatial Allocation in Transition

The distortions of the transition economy have been put into formal models by Gaddy, Ickes and others and have become widely known under the expression 'the virtual economy'[46]. The models focus on the non-monetary elements in the transition economy, their causes and consequences. The basic mechanism explained is the transfer of value from value-adding viable enterprises to low or negative value-adding only seemingly viable enterprises. This transfer of value occurs through barter transactions and money surrogates like veksels and debt offsets[47]. By this, economic transactions lose transparency and in effect output prices for these inefficient enterprises are above market prices and input prices below market prices. Hence, the Russian economy again faces a distorted price mechanism. It is obvious that these practices block restructuring of enterprises and reallocation among industries. The reasons for these practices can be found on the one hand in the fact that enterprise directors do not have an incentive to close down inefficient enterprises because they wish to keep their own position. On the other hand, massive restructuring and sectoral reallocation incurs enormous social costs which poses an incentive to the state to avoid restructuring. Consequently, government pushes the incentives of value-adding enterprises to engage in non-monetary transactions.

Among the non-monetary transactions is payment in kind for workers which worsens the income situation of households which had already become critical during the transition due to price liberalization. Given the loss in income, households had to develop strategies to cope with this situation. Among the strategies discussed are the acceptance of more than one job per family member, entrepreneurship and subsistence-oriented production of food on small plots and

46 For a theoretical analysis of the virtual economy see Ericson & Ickes, 2000, Gaddy and Ickes 1999a, 1999b and Gaddy 1999; for empirical analysis see Ivanenko 2001.

47 For specification of barter in the Russian economy see Commander & Mumssen 1998 and Guriev and Ickes (1999).

datchas[48]. Though the latter already played a role during Soviet times, its importance has increased in transition and now plays a significant role in food production.

These phenomena have considerable impact on the development of prices as an allocation mechanism and subsequently on reallocation and location structure. This view is backed by the fact that the economy in the Soviet Union was spatially highly segmented. A clear dichotomy between rural and urban areas can be stated. While in western industrialized economies the traditional dichotomy of rural and urban areas has been blurred during the last century, political intention in the Soviet Union kept the spatial organization of urban industrial and rural agricultural functions alive[49]. Hence, the situation in rural areas is very critical as alternatives to agriculture are scarce because industrial production and services are almost entirely concentrated in towns. Thereby some industries are concentrated in one plant in only one location and, furthermore, some cities and towns are almost entirely dependent on a single enterprise. As different branches of the economy are affected by elements of the virtual economy to a different degree, the impact of this factor reveals a transition pattern that corresponds to the spatial organization of the economy.

3.5.1 Vertical Integration in the Russian Agro-Food Sector

Agriculture is among the most severely affected branches in the economy. After price liberalization a gap between prices for inputs of agricultural production and farm-gate prices for agricultural production emerged that led to loss-making among agricultural enterprises and severely aggravated their financial state. As a consequence of this phenomenon and as a consequence of the regular delay in payments, which is symptomatic of the Russian economy, agents along the whole food processing chain started to integrate forward employing food processing and direct sales as cash generators.

The theory of industrial organization provides basically three determinants of vertical integration: technological economies, transactional economies and market imperfections[50]. It is questionable whether these factors provide a framework to describe and explain vertical integration in the Russian economy, because they have been identified for industries in mature market economies. Technology and subsequently technological economies are independent of economic systems and

48 Tho Seeth, 1995; Earle & Sakova, 1999.
49 Ioffe & Nefedova, 1997.
50 Perry in: Schmalensee & Willig (1989) p. 187.

would lead to vertical integration in either organization of an economy. Production processes are vertically integrated if the control over these processes lies in one responsibility and if the product is entirely consumed in the next stage in the production chain. This can be explained by technological economies if similarities occur along the production processes, which allow sharing in the means of production. Given the very different nature of agricultural production and food processing, vertical integration due to technological economies is not expected. It exists though in the Russian food industry and has gained important significance. Hence, the reasons have to be found in transaction costs and market imperfections.

Melyukhina & Khramova (in Wehrheim et al., 2000, p. 387 ff) describe the changes in food marketing in Russia during transition. Before the reforms the food economy revealed a rather simple pattern. Agricultural production was delivered to processing plants by collective farms. The linkages between the enterprises were determined by planners, i.e. enterprises could not choose their partners. Processing plants delivered their production either to storage facilities or to retailing. Outside this line existed food production by households, which was mainly subsistence-oriented. Some parts of this production were sold in local retail markets or to the collective farm. With transition a shift in significance of these two elements occurred. The share of household production in total production has significantly increased though their absolute production fell. Furthermore, with transition food imports at all stages of the food chain from processing to retail appeared. Moreover, food processing emerged at all stages of the chain. The share of on-farm processing in total processed output amounts to 47.9 per cent for meat, 14.1 per cent for milk products and 15.2 per cent for wheat flour.

The basic reasons given to explain vertical integration are the delays in payment, i.e. partners are not reliable and transactions become costly, the above mentioned price gap and the subsequent cash-creating incentive[51]. It seems plausible to explain this type of vertical integration by transaction costs economies which would be in line with a market economy approach. Nevertheless, the integration of processing and retailing is the result of a situation where markets were not in place and the distortions of the Soviet system fell under the rule of liberalized prices. Hence, the price gap between input prices and farm-gate prices for agricultural production.

---

51 Wandel in: Wehrheim et al. (2000) pp. 369, 371; Melyukhina & Khramova in: Wehrheim et al. (2000) pp. 387 ff.

3.5.2 Barter

Barter has not appeared to as significant an extent in the Russian economy at the beginning of transition as one could expect. Rather, a continuous rise in non-monetary transactions can only be stated since 1994[52]. It encompasses all kinds of transactions that enterprises are involved in: with other enterprises, with federal, regional and local governments, and with workers. As Guriev and Ickes (1999a, p. 5) state, barter differs across industries but the differences are not statistically significant.

However, the same study reveals a factor for the use of barter transactions which is very much linked to the type of industry, that is market concentration and distance to market. It turns out that consumer industries or industries which tend to have closer contact with consumers are less likely to have a high share of barter transactions than more upstream industries, and that a high share of barter transactions is more likely in concentrated markets. Furthermore, a relation between firm size and share of barter seems likely. These three arguments fit well together as enterprises near to the consumer are likely to be smaller and are less concentrated. It is necessary to mention that barter is not a question of yes or no, but that most enterprises use a combination of barter and money exchanges where the share of barter ranges from 10 per cent to 90 per cent.

Table 3-3: Share of Barter in Sales of Different Industries

Industry	Number of enterprises in the sample	Share of barter in sales in November 1998	
		Weighted average	Std. Deviation
Electricity	4	0,67	0,12
Fuel	6	0,21	0,23
Ferrous metals	32	0,50	0,19
Non-ferrous metals	6	0,26	0,19
Chemical and petrochemical	44	0,46	0,21
Machinery	307	0,48	0,23
Pulp and forestry	75	0,47	0,23
Construction materials	71	0,51	0,22
Textile	164	0,43	0,25
Food	82	0,28	0,21
Other	15	0,17	0,18
Total	806	0,44	0,24

Source: Guriev & Ickes, 1999, p. 6

52 Commander & Mumssen, 1998, p. 1.

3.5.3 Wage Arrears

One form of barter is payment in kind to workers. However, sometimes workers are not paid at all. Like barter transactions between enterprises, the phenomenon of wage arrears emerged at the beginning of transition but became critical in the later years until 1996 as shown in table 3-4. The continuation of wage arrears over a long period is possible because there is an incentive for entrepreneurs to keep workers on the payroll as much as there is an incentive for workers to stay on the payroll.

Enterprises had a weak incentive to restructure also due to political decisions. Government renders costly the restructuring of enterprises in order to avoid the social costs of unemployment. For example, according to Russian law, enterprises had to pay three months severance pay to workers who lost their jobs because of workforce reduction[53]. As a result, enterprises chose to keep their workforce and not to pay wages in full, in time or at all. Workers have an incentive to accept wage arrears because they benefit from being on the payroll through services like cheap housing, schooling, day-care services etc. Hence, they preferred to be not paid but profit from the services rather than to become unemployed.

Table 3-4: Wage Arrears in Different Sectors of the Economy

Trends in Sectoral Wage Arrears			
(1) Outstanding wage arrears (billions of December 1995 rubles)			
	Industry	Construction	Agriculture
1992	1034	541	397
1993	2653	840	2092
1994	5019	1686	3009
1995	7734	1941	2571
1996	18185	5310	4855
(2) Ratio of outstanding wage arrears to the monthly wage bill (per cent)			
1992	5	6	6
1993	13	10	36
1994	31	23	68
1995	61	40	102
1996	111	74	158

Source: Desai & Idson, 1998a, p.

That leads to another point that Desai & Idson (1998b) examine in an empirical study. The distribution of wage arrears is unequal among workers, industries and regions. As managers would risk losing their most productive workers as al-

53 Desai & Idson, 1998a, p.4.

ternative jobs for these workers might exist, they tend to withhold wages from less qualified and low paid workers but pay the skilled workers in full. It should be noted that managers by this revealed market oriented behaviour rather than equity guided behaviour as stemming from a planned economy. Moreover, table 3-4 additionally illustrates that there is a clear distinction between sectors of the economy. Though in absolute terms less affected, the most severely affected sector of the economy is agriculture given that wages are much lower here. Moreover, workers living in poor regions are more likely to be affected by withholding of wages than workers in richer regions.

3.5.4 Summary

The bread industry which is of interest in the present study belongs to consumer good industries. It is a fragmented industry which is very close to the consumer. Hence, only a limited influence of barter transactions can be expected at first sight. On the other hand, bread belongs to the food industry where vertical integration plays a significant role. However, bread can on the one hand be subject to this vertical integration by grain producing enterprises, and on the other hand bread can also be produced by small bakeries that are independent of grain producing enterprises.

Furthermore, the discussion of wage arrears has shown that agriculture is much more affected than other economic sectors. As wages in agriculture are much lower than wages in industry or services, and the probability of payment in kind is thus much higher for agricultural workers, and as the strong dichotomy between rural and urban areas exists, the influence of transition phenomena on reallocation in the bread industry can be summarized as follows: rural area means agriculture, wage arrears and vertical integration, i.e. markets cannot develop because there is no monetary economy; urban areas means industry, less extent of wage arrears and no vertical integration, i.e. markets can develop because bread is close to the consumer who is independent of the producer and money prices are paid.

3.6 Conclusions

The preceding sub-sections derived the organization of the bread industry in the same regional setting under two different economic regimes. Due to differences in assumptions, the resulting patterns differed significantly from each other. The discussion of the allocation processes in each case started from a plane field, i.e.

a region where there is no bread production at all. The ideas deriving from these discussions will conclude with hypotheses on the question: what happens if the new allocation mechanism meets an existing structure under the conditions of the 'virtual economy'.

3.6.1 The Transition Process

Assuming that the command system has functioned perfectly and each consumer was supplied the amount of bread needed, the question arises whether there is scope for changes. It is, if a new entity can produce at a lower cost than the old entities. As has become clear from section 3.2.4, the overestimation of fixed costs in the long run by planners has led to the conclusion that production in large entities is cheaper while in the market economy fixed costs are negligible in the long run and bread production shows constant returns to scale and no economies of scale. Old enterprises are now faced with this new cost situation. According to this assumption all enterprises produce at the same cost. Hence, transportation costs cannot be offset by decreasing average production costs. As a result, all settlements that are of a minimum size for viability of a bakery and which are supplied with bread from an outside production facility are a business opportunity[54]. Given that at the beginning a new enterprise and an old enterprise compete for the market, marginal cost pricing is plausible. However, the old enterprise had to price marginal cost plus transportation cost and is not competitive. Subsequently, old enterprises withdraw from these markets. This process starts in more distant markets. In the rural areas there are settlements left with a population below the minimum scale of viability for a bakery. As new enterprises have started to develop in these areas, they in some cases lie closer to these settlements than the old enterprises and, again due to transportation costs, old enterprises have to withdraw from this market, too. Once the old enterprises have withdrawn from the distant markets they served, the equity in production costs no longer holds due to overcapacities in capital and workforce[55]. A new enterprise working at full

---

54 In a regional setting like this enterprises in more distant locations are likely to face higher transportation costs on the input side. However, it is plausible to assume that the transportation costs on the input side are much lower than the transportation costs of the produce as the main input is storable and can be delivered in higher amounts than fresh bread.

55 According to the planned scenario old enterprises in towns and cities have produced for this settlement and it is not likely to assume that they have delivered. However, as planners preferred to deliver rather than to tie up new capital, it is more likely to assume that all enterprises had to supply surrounding areas with bread.

capacity now has a cost advantage over the old enterprises. As a result, new bakeries can start competing at the production locations of old enterprises in cities and towns.

However, this scenario assumes that economic behaviour, i.e. the opening of bakeries, reaches distant areas at the same time as the information that a market economy is in place. This is unlikely as learning new forms of behaviour is a long process which depends on observation and experience. Still, the opening of bread producing facilities firstly in distant areas can be expected due to two reasons: the likelihood of underprovision in Soviet reality and the vertical integration argument. Agricultural enterprises had to react to the new price relation very quickly, and hence the opening of processing can be expected at an early stage in transition.

Hypotheses that can be drawn so far:

The first bakeries appear in distant settlements with minimum scale for viability. Along with this process goes the decline in production of old entities. Later, bakeries in towns emerge and a competitive market develops. The driving factors are distance, demand and overcapacities.

3.6.2 The Enterprise Population

The logical consequence of competition in cities and towns would be that old enterprises either reduce their capacities or are completely driven out of the market. However, at this stage the transition scenario according to section 3.4.2 sets in. In order to avoid the social costs of reducing their workforce old enterprises start engaging in strategies of 'the virtual economy' and stay in the market, accepting market prices and setting off their losses through blurring non-monetary transactions. Consequently, old enterprises would make up one group of enterprises. A second group would be commercial bakeries, while the bakeries opened on agricultural enterprises could make up two groups:

Grain producing enterprises integrate vertically to receive cash. For this incentive they would try to sell their production also at other locations. The ability to do so depends on their position relative to large settlements. As they have a strong liquidity constraint, their production costs are also blurred through barter, wage arrears etc. and they take market prices. Given this scenario the building of new capacities in the bread sector would not be driven only by demand and, therefore, not be proportional to the necessary capacities. Hence, an overrepresentation of bakeries in grain producing areas can be expected.

Agricultural enterprises which are not mainly grain producers, or which lie distant from large settlements, face the same financial situation. As they are not able to pay their workers they try to supply them with necessary food items. Hence, they process their agricultural production and distribute it among their workers and install a bakery to serve the population with bread. It is possibly easier and cheaper for them to install a bakery than to distribute money as they might be able to achieve necessary inputs through non-monetary transactions and they are able to offset wage arrears with provision of food items. While this capacity building might be in compliance with demand it can hardly be regarded as market development.

According to the above discussion the following types of enterprise are expected to constitute the enterprise population:

- Old enterprises which cannot be assigned to market oriented enterprises as they follow survival strategies which lead to inefficiencies in the industry.
- Agricultural enterprises which form a subsistence economy at the level of the enterprises which comprise all settlements assigned to the enterprise. These facilities cannot be regarded as market-oriented.
- Agricultural enterprises that have vertically integrated and produce bread to sell in markets for cash. Though production is oriented to markets, in a strict sense these units cannot be regarded as market-oriented.
- Small new enterprises whose activity is exclusively bread production. Due to their young age they do not have the opportunity to engage in non-monetary transactions. They pay market prices for inputs and sell at market prices. Their activity leads either to zero-profits or is profitable. Loss-making bakeries are driven out of the market in the long run. They can be regarded as market-oriented.

3.6.3 The Spatial Organization of the Industry

As the hypotheses on the enterprise population already indicate, the transition process is expected to lead to a rural-urban distribution of markets where some kind of market develops in the urban area that can broadly be described as functioning by the interplay of supply and demand. In some parts of the rural areas a subsistence economy develops and between these two lies a belt where agricultural enterprises sell in markets, employing their own inputs and paying their workers in kind.

However, a simple two- or threefold distinction of areas is not sufficient as the structure of markets and their functioning is also of great interest. The discussion in chapter 3.3.2 revealed market size as the determining factor for the number and size of enterprises in the markets and showed a negative relationship between market size and concentration. Hence, in large markets a huge number of equally sized firms is expected, while in small markets monopolies are expected.

At this point again the transition factors set in. In the case of developing market structure the already existing and remaining production units are crucial. In large markets enterprises are already operating. These enterprises will try to prevent entry of new enterprises. In any case they will continue production. As a consequence, the following market structures can be expected:

- In urban markets a structure of a dominant firm with a fringe will emerge. The number of new entries depends on the power of old enterprises to prevent new entries.
- In small markets that are not entirely involved in agriculture, monopolies or duopolies will emerge according to the market-size-market-structure rule where the normal functioning of a monopoly market can be expected.
- Where agricultural enterprises operate that enter urban markets to earn cash, the market-size-market-structure rule can be distorted. Though it is likely that in this case only small settlements and hence small markets are involved, the expected monopoly might emerge but the capacities of these entities can be distorted by the intention to sell production in urban markets.
- In settlements that entirely belong to an agricultural enterprise that has vertically integrated, the market-size-market-structure rule can also be distorted. In this case it is sufficient for the agricultural enterprise to establish a bakery with the capacity to serve the market. While the capacity building is still in compliance with demand, the market structure is not: in a large market a single enterprise could emerge or the agricultural enterprise could decide to place the bakery in a small settlement due to random factors (existing facilities etc.).

3.6.4 Prices

Due to the different purposes of the production units, the spatial patterns of prices can differ significantly from an expected market economy pattern. Given the distribution from a competitive market in urban areas to a monopoly in small settlements, prices are going to increase from the former to the latter. However, in the transition scenario the relation can be expected to be the other way round: agricultural enterprises that operate bakeries in the potential monopolies produce with the purpose of supplying their workers in lieu of wages. They are going to price on a production cost basis while enterprises in a competitive environment have to price above production costs to gain some profit.

The hypotheses are summarized in figure 3-5.

Figure 3-5: Spatial Allocation of the Bread Industry under the Conditions of a Transition Economy

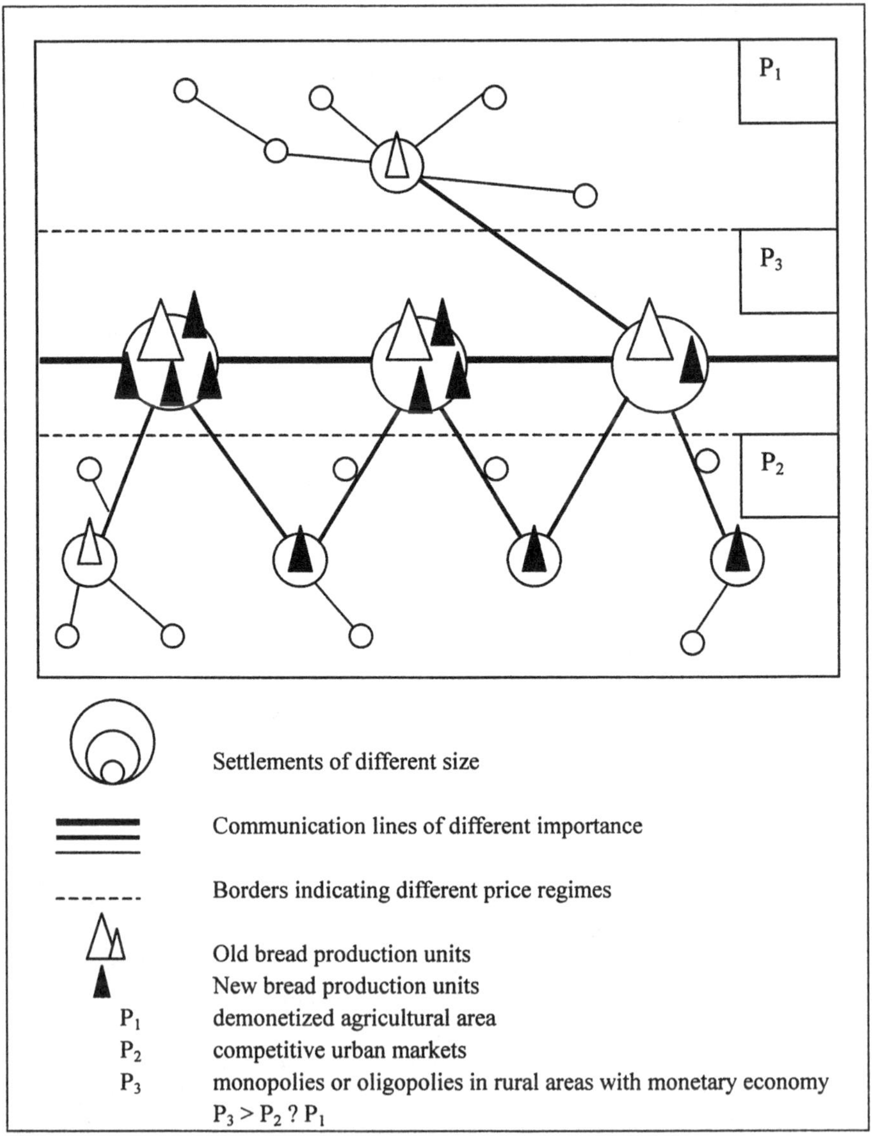

Source: author's own drawing

4. The Course of Transition in the Spatial Pattern of the Bread Industry in the Irkutsk Oblast

4.1 Introduction

The discussion in chapter three resulted in hypotheses on three issues: the process of reallocation itself, the resulting enterprise population and the resulting markets. These three dimensions of the transition of a single industry will be treated separately in the next chapters. The objective of this chapter is to describe and to explain the course of transition in the bread industry in the Irkutsk Oblast. In the first subsection the analysis aims to answer the questions: what happened, where and when in the bread sector in the Irkutsk Oblast and who was involved while the second subsection assesses the role and direction of impact of the determining factors.

For the description and explanation of the process, it is necessary to clearly fix the beginning of the transition period. Although restrictions on private businesses had already been relaxed by the mid- 1980's, and new entities emerged between 1985 and 1991, for the present purpose the year of price liberalization, 1992, is taken as the beginning of the transition process. To fix the number of bread baking facilities at the beginning of transition the official statistics serve as the basic source of information. There are 19 large- and medium- sized units counted, out of which 3 were founded between 1991 and 1995 as shown in table 4-1.

Table 4-1: Distribution of Large and Medium Scale Bakeries by the Year of Foundation

Total number	Year of foundation									
	pre 1941	1941-1950	1951-1960	1961-1970	1971-1980	1981-1990	1991-1995	1996	1997	1998
19	4	1	5	4	1	1	3	-	-	-

Source: Committee for State Statistics in the Irkutsk Oblast, 1999, p. 5

Hence, the actual number cannot be established and, as a result, 17 entities are taken as the basis. This number of bread factories is in compliance with old bread enterprises registered in Business Karta, a private index of enterprises in the Russian regions which also names the date of foundation of the enterprises. Entities that do not belong to the regions covered by the study are excluded. This information is compiled from the information from the survey, which partly covered the old large units. Through this information, enterprises could be detected that were founded much earlier but give the year of privatization as the year of foundation. All of the enterprises are located in cities and towns.

Additionally smaller entities existed which are not mentioned in the official statistics. The survey revealed 32 units, which do not belong to the group of officially named large bread factories but are older than 1992. Except for three units, all of these facilities are located in villages of different sizes. Furthermore, some of the new bakeries were founded on the basis of an old production unit and hence were included into the list of locations in 1992.

At the beginning of the transition period bread was produced in 62 production facilities distributed over 54 locations. Out of these, five locations had more than one production unit. By 2000, there were 261 enterprises at 145 production locations: 17 old production facilities that are not completely covered by the survey, 32 old small entities subsequently referred to as the old additional system which were identified by the survey, and 212 new entities which were identified by the survey.

Table 4-2: Number of Bread Production Entities and Number of Locations in 1992 and 2000.

	At the beginning of the transition process, 1992	By the year 2000
Number of bread production entities	62	261
Number of locations where bread is produced	54	145

Source: Business Karta, 1999; Survey 2000; Committee for State Statistics in the Irkutsk Oblast, 1999, p. 5

From this information some brief conclusions can already be drawn that should serve as the starting point for further analysis. From the discussions of the planned economy and market economy allocation mechanisms described in chapter three, the prediction was made that during transition the old enterprises will continue to operate while the number of bread production facilities, as well as the number of locations where production takes place, will increase. This prediction is supported by the observations in table 4-2. After eight years of transition, a significantly higher number of production units is operating and the spatial distribution is much more dispersed than in the planned economy situation. Moreover, there is no evidence that old large facilities have vanished, while parts of the old additional system were substituted by new enterprises. However, this brief conclusion needs a deeper discussion. It is necessary to estimate whether the capacity building and reallocation is in compliance with the market economy, i.e. demand, or whether the factors mentioned in section 3.5 interfere with this process.

The present chapter is dedicated to analyzing the three groups of factors that explain the course of spatial reallocation in bread production. Therefore, it concentrates on the emergence of new entities rather than on capacity building. The partly contradictory factors can be summed up in one group of market factors where the direction of cost argument contradicts the direction of the behavioral aspects of learning market economic behavior and the transitional aspects, which distort the demand-driven explanation of reallocation.

The process that will be described and explained is the dispersion of bread production, which means its spreading through space over a certain period of time. This is equivalent to the idea of diffusion. Hence, the following step in the analysis borrows its theoretical background from diffusion theory. Additionally, this approach allows combining the different overlaying patterns of explanation.

4.2 Reallocation in Bread Production as a Diffusion Process

4.2.1 The Diffusion of Market Economic Behaviour

The crucial point in analysing diffusion processes is to clearly define the innovation, the potential adopters and their decision-making, and the information flow[56]. In the framework here the diffusion of the market economy is under consideration. Although the macroeconomic conditions might change all of a sudden, the implementation in individual behaviour and decision-making is a lagged process. If the market economy diffuses over time and space, it is assumed that some settlements are reached later than others.

The innovation in the context here is not bread-baking which is known and might already be established at the location in the form of a plant. The innovation is the opening of a business by an individual. The individual can either be a private person or a private enterprise. Since each settlement of minimum size represents a market, it can be expected that at the end of the diffusion process at least one commercial bakery is established in all these settlements.

Opening a business comprises different actions such as: a) the information about the possibility of opening a bakery reaches the individual (**information spread**); b) the individual recognizes opening a bakery as a profitable economic activity that suits his situation (**economic opportunity**); c) The individual de-

56 Coombs et al., 1987, p. 121.

cides to open a bakery (**enterprise emergence**). These steps are described below[57].

a) Information spread

How the information about an innovation reaches an individual depends on the type of innovation, the communication infrastructure and the question whether there is an agent who promotes distribution or whether it diffuses without a motor[58]. An innovation could be a product or a production technology. For products there is usually an agent who has an interest in selling it, and therefore will promote it among the individuals who are possible adopters. In the case of a new production technology, the circle of possible adopters is limited and the agent starts promoting where his or her costs are least, or his or her expected profits are maximum. Other innovations like behaviour or cultures do not have a promoter. They diffuse through contacts between individuals, for example tourists with the population of a tourist region.

These different types of diffusion also have spatial aspects[59]. For a product such as television, all households or individuals are possible adopters. A promoter might expect most profits in areas where he can reach the highest number of potential adopters with limited costs of advertising and marketing, while he might avoid other areas completely where he does not expect a minimum number of adopters. In a society where communications infrastructure is highly developed and information can easily be transported, the promoter would start in cities and then go to less populated areas. At the same time the information about the new product diffuses into areas the promoter would not touch through contacts between individuals who then seek to adopt the innovation. It comes to simultaneity by different diffusion mechanisms.[60]

For major changes like the breakdown of a political and economic system, there exist central information sources which distribute the information. Since television and radio are available almost everywhere in Russia, it is assumed that

57 Rogers (1962) set the base for the understanding of innovation diffusion with his concept of different types of adopters like ‘pioneers’, ‘early imitators’ and ‘laggards’.

58 See Brown, 1981, for an overview of different approaches to innovation diffusion in space and time. He distinguishes between the adoption approach which is solely oriented on demand, the market and infrastructure approach which is supply driven, the economic history approach and the development approach.

59 See Fischer in Anderson et al., 1989, pp. 55-57 for an overview; Hägerstrand, 1967, for the basic work on spatial diffusion.

60 Windhorst, 1983.

the information about the changes reached all parts of the population and all regions with little time lag.

b) Economic opportunity

That the information has reached a possible adopter does not mean that the individual recognizes the benefits of the innovation and immediately decides to adopt it. For example, all enterprises can be seen as possible adopters of a new accounting software, but not all enterprises might see the benefits of the new one compared to the old one given the fact that it incurs costs and requires a learning process. In addition, individual characteristics might also have an impact on the adoption decision. Some individuals prefer to wait until others have tried it out, or they need more time to understand all aspects of the innovation.

Adopting a market economy means accepting new parameters, learning new rules and understanding the consequences of one's behaviour when these new rules are applied. This also comprises understanding the possibilities and dangers of the new system. Each individual is a possible adopter of market economic behaviour[61].

The diffusion of this learning process can be expected to be very much spatial. Learning processes are guided by either trial and error or repetition or observation. It can be expected that an individual does not learn all features of the new system with the first contact, although some parts of life are strongly affected all of a sudden. The more contact an individual has compared to other individuals in applying the new rules, using the opportunities they offer and coping with the situation, the earlier he/she is ready to adopt this behaviour. In a spatial sense the diffusion of market economic behaviour is expected to be a hierarchical process through the settlement system. The chances to observe market economic behaviour are much higher in centres where more economic activity is located and more individuals with experience in a market economy are present.

c) Enterprise emergence

Although each individual is a possible adopter of market economic behaviour, only a limited number express it by opening a bakery. It requires interest and knowledge or the willingness to acquire appropriate knowledge. Here it is assumed that the number of individuals able and willing to open a bakery is proportional to the population at a location and evenly distributed.

61 Kapur, 1995.

Finally, the decision to open a bakery demands some prerequisites, which do not lie in the individual's abilities or motivation. Although an individual has the ability and the willingness to open a bakery, he/she might decide not to do so because of the administrative and financial difficulties he/she faces which depend on his/her risk aversion. It is assumed that the factors hampering the adoption are equally distributed over space.

4.2.2 Bread Baking as a Survival Strategy

In the transition economy, the diffusion process discussed above could be overlaid by the phenomenon of vertical integration which can be seen as a survival strategy for agricultural enterprises. It can be assumed *a priori* that this process will be dominant in rural areas irrespective of the distance to urban centres, and hence the opportunity to observe market economic behaviour.

As price liberalization led to a liquidity crisis all of a sudden, and for almost all agricultural enterprises at the same time, all enterprises had to react at almost the same time to guarantee their survival. The establishment of bakeries to process their own raw materials and sell it either in markets or to their own workers is consequently a reaction that is not spatial in the sense that diffusion depends on distances but covers all enterprises over a very short period of time.

4.3 Diffusion Model for the Emergence of Bread Baking Facilities during Transition

Geroski (2000) describes different diffusion models for technical innovations. While epidemic models are based on the assumption that adoption occurs with getting the information, probit models define certain thresholds like expected profits that need to be passed to initiate adoption. By this, probit models take differences in the capabilities and goals of the individuals into account. While the former model is suited for situations where the innovation is very easy to adopt, the latter model better describes the situation of choice between alternatives.

The discussion above assumes a diffusion process through space which is determined by two mechanisms that are contrary to each other. Therefore, two groups of population are distinguished. The first represents all urban population, and the second all rural population. Since the economy was spatially segmented, these two populations are statistically easy to identify with around 80 per cent urban and 20 per cent rural.[62] It is expected that all the 20 per cent of rural population are covered by agricultural enterprises[63], and therefore the number of possible adopters is given by the number of grain- producing enterprises. The remaining 80 per cent urban population lives in towns and cities of different sizes.

For the rural population, the diffusion is quite easy to identify. An epidemic model with a central information source can describe it. Price liberalization and the gap between input and output prices hit all enterprises approximately at the same time and forced them to react at approximately the same time. According to Geroski (2000, p. 606) the course of diffusion in rural areas can be described as follows:

$$y(t) = N[1 - \exp\{-\alpha t\}]$$

where $y(t)$ represents the number of enterprises which have adopted at a given point of time, N the Number of potential adopters which is equivalent to the number of grain producing enterprises, and finally α the percentage of enterprises reached by the information source in each period, i.e. the speed of the diffusion process.

The epidemic model is criticized because it does not sufficiently account for the slow speed of many diffusion processes[64]. The adoption of an innovation cannot be explained by the provision of information about the innovation, as many diffusion processes are much slower. However, in the context here the epidemic model is applicable for several reasons. It provides equations for the course of diffusion which is more important here than the expected speed. For the present analysis it is hypothesized that the overlaying processes in the rural areas distort the normal s-curve course of diffusion. Furthermore, it is assumed that adopting market economic behavior is a learning process which depends on the number of contacts with the respective behavior when other factors are equally distributed. Therefore, the epidemic model serves also for the second group[65].

Finding an appropriate model for the second group is more difficult since the decision-makers are individuals for whom opening a bakery might be one alternative among others. As mentioned above, the innovation is a change in behavior, which is reached by a learning process. Each individual has to go through this

62 Committee for State Statistics in the Irkutsk Oblast, 1997, p. 5.

63 The kolchoses and sowchoses of the Soviet System usually comprised several villages which inhabitants worked as agricultural or technical staff on the farms.

64 Geroski, 2000; Coombs et al., 1987, p. 124.

65 Andersen (1999) confirms the s-shaped curve for long-term evolution paths of individual technologies.

process and to react to the new situation in some way. A private person in this situation can choose between continuing his/her old work, finding a new better-paid job or starting a business. In the case of the unemployed the same holds true. Whether the person opens a bakery or starts any other business depends on the abilities or interests of the person. Therefore, it is assumed that the number of possible adopters is a certain percentage of the population, exactly the part who have the ability and interest to open a bakery. Furthermore, the number of bakeries in one market is limited by demand, which is represented by population and by income.[66] Here it is assumed that the learning process of the individual does not play a role whether it observes success in the business it would open itself or in any other business. The diffusion process is determined by the expectation of the individual to be successful in the business and to gain greater income than by continuing work. The expectation rises with decreasing risk aversion and with an increasing number of positive observations in opening a business. Here the usual assumption is that the degree of risk aversion is normally distributed and does not reveal a spatial pattern and that the number of observations of successful businesses is higher in bigger cities than in smaller cities. Therefore, the second diffusion process can be described as the usual s-curve diffusion summed up over all cities and towns with a time lag that becomes longer the smaller the town. The mixed information source model as described by Geroski can give this.

$$Y(t) = N\{1 - \exp[-(\alpha/\sigma)t]\} \times \{1 + \psi \exp[-(\beta/\sigma)]\}^{-1},$$

where $\sigma = \alpha/(\alpha+k)$ represents the relative strength of the common information source which is necessary to start the diffusion process with $k = \beta N$. β expresses the probability that each adopter contacts an individual that has not yet adopted, i.e. word of mouth diffusion. The ratio of potential users to users is expressed by ψ.

Figure 4-1 gives a more detailed impression of the idea. The lower panel of figure 4-1a) represents the quick forced adjustment process of agricultural enterprises which account for 20 per cent of the population, while the upper panel of figure 4-1a) shows the diffusion in the urban population. Figure 4-1b) is the sum of both graphs and reveals a diminished s-curve of the diffusion process.

66 Bread might not be a very income-elastic commodity and therefore income might not be an appropriate variable. However, enterprises in the region reported quick reactions to demand on constraints in income. For example, the interviews were conducted at the time when people had to buy textbooks for their children. Bakeries explained a simultaneous decrease in demand by this fact.

Figure 4-1: Expected Course of Diffusion of Bakeries during Transition

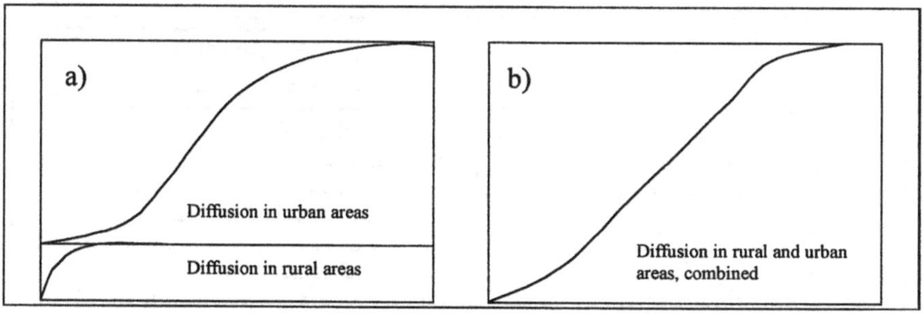

Source: author's own drawing adapted from Geroski, 2000.

The model of a combined diffusion process results in a diminished s-shaped diffusion curve. To show whether the model correctly predicts the diffusion of bakeries in the Irkutsk Oblast during the transition, two curves are constructed based on the actual numbers. Figure 4-2 shows the emergence of new bakeries in the Irkutsk Oblast starting in 1992. The curve indicates that the process is not yet finished. To base the calculations for the predicted curve with the right number of possible adopters, the assumption is made that the downward slope that has already been reached continues with the same speed until the process is over and all possible adopters have adopted. The total number of new bakeries is then about 220.

However, to ease the calculations the total population is reduced to 200 adopters. To calculate the predicted curve the enterprise population is divided into 40 adopters for the rural part and 160 adopters for the urban part. Calculations are made according to the equations given in the preceding sections. Figure 4-3 shows the predicted curve as calculated by the equations discussed and the actual curve as it was observed in the Irkutsk Oblast. Both curves have almost exactly the same shape. The third graph in the figure shows the curve of a normal epidemic diffusion to reveal the difference between both processes. It can be concluded that the combined epidemic diffusion model describes the diffusion of bakeries in the Irkutsk Oblast. Hence, the prediction is strengthened that transition phenomena have a distorting impact on reallocation in bread production. The figures 1-10 in the appendix show the spatial distribution of bakeries through the Irkutsk Oblast.

Figure: 4-2: Emergence of New Bakeries in the Irkutsk Oblast during Transition

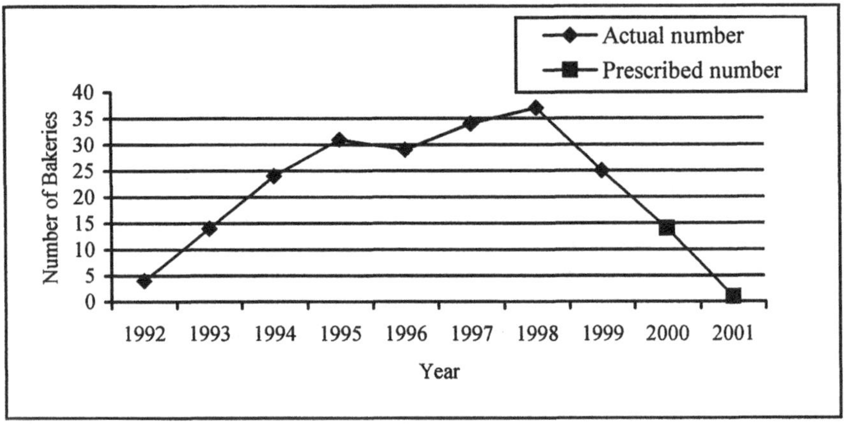

Source: Survey 2000; author's own calculations.

Figure: 4-3: Cumulative Number of New Bakeries in the Irkutsk Oblast during Transition

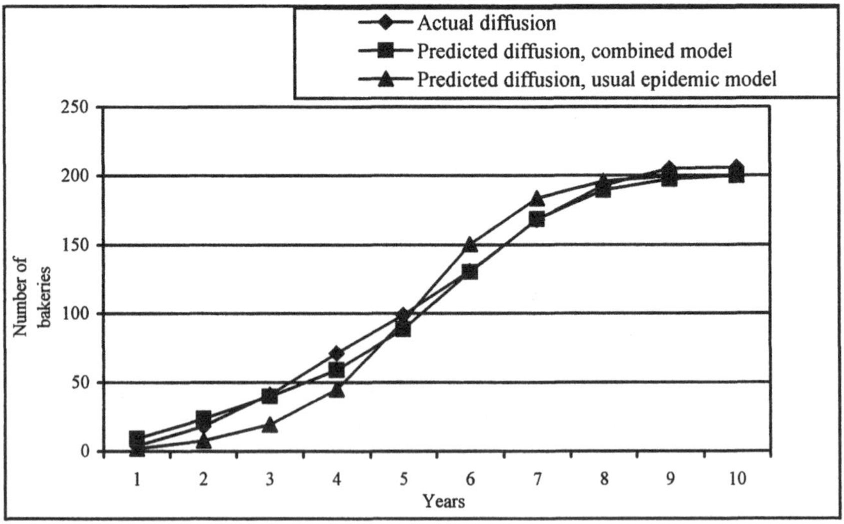

Source: Survey 2000; author's own calculations.

4.4 Determinants of the Diffusion of Bread Baking

In the preceding sections a model was presented that describes the emergence of bread baking facilities in the Irkutsk Oblast as a combination of two overlaying processes which in time dimension and spatial direction are in contrast to each other. The predicted course of transition with weighted mechanisms in rural and urban areas has been supported by the course as it was observed in the Irkutsk Oblast in the respective time period. However, this model merely represents a description of the transition course. Although its prediction is based on theoretical considerations, it does not allow for conclusions on the determinants of the process. Detecting these requires further analytical steps.

4.4.1 Determinants and Estimation

Analyzing determinants of spatial phenomena incurs several statistical problems which are crucial in the present case. These are spatial autocorrelation and spatial heterogeneity.[67] In the discussion above spatial heterogeneity was excluded theoretically by assuming that risk aversion and the ability to open a bakery are equally distributed over space, and hence behavior is spatially independent. However, the problem of spatial autocorrelation remains.

As illustrated in the preceding section, the transition course of spatial reallocation of bread production in the Irkutsk Oblast is assumed to be composed of two mechanisms of which one is hypothesized to be purely transitional while the other is hypothesized to be market driven. Regarding the spatial aspect, both mechanisms bear different characteristics. While the transitional mechanism represents a reaction to a changing economic environment and is spatial only in the urban-rural context, the market oriented mechanism is spatial in itself, i.e. what happens at one location depends on what happens in other locations. Regarding the example of bread production, market-oriented bakeries are going to open where there is room in the market and not where the market is already occupied. It is important to note that this dependence is not only in the spatial dimension but also in the time dimension, i.e. the establishment of production facilities last year impact on the establishment of production facilities this year. Consequently, this part of the model can be expected to be highly autocorrelated.

Furthermore, the analysis has to determine both mechanisms simultaneously. One difficulty lies in finding an appropriate endogenous variable as a diffusion mechanism is a process in space and time, i.e. the dependent variable should

67 Anselin, 1987.

characterize the where and the when. In the case of the survival mechanism, the when can be characterized by the year and the where by the fact that the operator is an agricultural enterprise or by the simple characterization of the location as rural. For the market mechanism the when is also easy to determine, while the where becomes more difficult. For example, the distance to the next center, i.e. the more distant the market the later a bakery appears, is an explanatory variable at the same time.

However, this problem can be avoided as, theoretically, the when is explained by the where, early in rural areas and in large centers, later in smaller urban centers. The following calculations are based on the year of emergence of bakeries as a dependent variable and distance is treated as exogenous. Two possibilities exist: to base the analysis on spatial units, i.e. locations or districts and to explain when bakeries appeared or secondly, to base the analysis on the bakeries and to explain by their characteristics and the characteristics of their location when they appeared. While in the first case serial correlation could cause problems, because the endogenous variable is based on spatial units, in the second case spatial autocorrelation can be avoided. Furthermore, the first approach delivers a rather crude result as distance variables cannot be included which are most important in accounting for the usual or market part of the diffusion process and, additionally, the sample is too small to produce robust results.

Moreover, problematic for the interpretation of the regression results is the fact that most of the available variables represent an early emergence of a bakery while variables for a late emergence of a bakery can hardly be given due to the aggregate nature of spatial units: in large cities bakeries are expected earlier than in smaller cities, and bakeries are expected to emerge early in agricultural areas. It is difficult to distinguish theoretically whether bakeries in agricultural areas are expected to emerge earlier than in large cities as the diffusion mechanisms overlay each other. As the second approach for a regression analysis is based on single bakeries, these problems can be accounted for.

However, for the second approach data availability is another problem because secondary data is available for large towns and districts but not separated for single municipalities. Hence, aggregate data has to be used as regressors for a regressand that is based on single entities.

4.4.2 Estimation Based on Spatial Units

The year when the first bakery emerged in the region serves as the regressand in an ordered probit model. This model was chosen because years do not represent a continuum with exact determination of point in time but rather order the observations in early, later and late emergence. The population consists of districts and large towns with a total number of observations of 35. Entities where until the year 2000 no bakery has emerged are represented by the year 2003, assuming that bakeries will appear.

Econometrically the emergence of the first firm in a town or district has to be expressed in rank order where ranks are ordinal and rank 0< rank 1 ...<rank 11, rank 0 representing the year 1992 and rank 11 representing the year 2003. A latent regression model follows[68]:

$$y^* = \beta' x + \varepsilon$$

Where y^* is emergence of the first bakery, which is unobserved. Observed is:

$$\begin{aligned} y &= 0 \; if \; y^* \leq 0 \\ &= 1 \; if \; 0 < y^* \leq \mu_1 \\ &= 2 \; if \; \mu_1 < y^* \leq \mu_2 \\ &= 3 \; if \; \mu_2 < y^* \leq \mu_3 \\ &= 4 \, if \; \mu_3 < y^* \leq \mu_4 \\ &= 5 \, if \; \mu_4 < y^* \leq \mu_5 \\ &= 6 \, if \; \mu_5 < y^* \leq \mu_6 \\ &= 7 \, if \; \mu_6 < y^* \leq \mu_7 \\ &= 8 \, if \; \mu_7 < y^* \leq \mu_8 \\ &= 9 \, if \; \mu_8 < y^* \leq \mu_9 \\ &= 10 \, if \; \mu_9 < y^* \leq \mu_{10} \\ &= 11 \; if \; \mu_{11} \leq y^* \end{aligned}$$

where μ are unknown parameters to be estimated with β, and x are observable characteristics of the spatial units as described below. Here, ε are unobservable factors. Assuming that ε is normally distributed with mean 0 and variance 1, the probabilities and corresponding marginal effects are estimated utilizing the ordered probit method.

---

68 Greene, 2000, pp. 875-877.

The regressors in the model on the one hand represent the market driven process, on the other hand the transition process. Furthermore, the rural-urban dimension is taken into account. The explanation for the choice of independent variables is given below:

Market mechanism:

- ***Population***: The population in the district or town is an important representative for demand in bread. However, in the context of the diffusion process it is difficult to interpret. Following the discussion of chapter three, enterprises are expected to emerge later than in rural areas because old enterprises in the market succeed in keeping their position in the market at the beginning of the process. On the other hand, business activities are much higher in larger towns and, consequently, bakeries can be expected to emerge at an early stage in the process. As this follows the market mechanism argument, the coefficient is expected to be negative (*Pop96*).
- ***Average income***: Constraints on purchasing power are a significant factor for enterprise development in transition countries. Consequently this variable is added. The coefficient is expected to be negative because it is expected that bakeries emerge first where income is higher. (*Inc95*).

Transition mechanism

- ***Area under grain production*** in the year 1995 serves as a proxy for the presence of grain producing enterprises, which are possible adopters for the quick transitional mechanism. The coefficient is expected to be negative as these bakeries are expected to be the first to emerge. (*Gra95*)
- ***Ratio of workforce on agricultural enterprises to the total workforce***: This variable is included to account for the influence on demand of the subsistence character of agricultural enterprises. The coefficient is expected to be negative because bakeries in areas where agricultural activity is high are expected to be the first to emerge (*Wfa*).
- ***Volume of wage arrears per worker in relation to the average income*** in 1997. The variable represents the transitional aspect of diffusion though its significance rose late in the transition process. Therefore the year 1997 was chosen. (*Dew97*)

Rural-urban dimension

- A rural-urban dummy is added to account for the two overlaying mechanisms. (*Rub*).

The summary statistics are shown in table 4-3.

Table 4-3: Summary Statistics; Dependent Variable: Year when First Bakery Emerged; Model: Ordered Probit

Regressor	Name	Mean	Standard deviation
Year when the first bakery emerged	First	3.2	3.4
Regressands			
Population at 01.01.1996	Pop96	67.98	108.61
Average monthly income per houshold in Roubles	In95	615.4	256.4
Area under grain production in 1995	Gra95	18979.7	19758.1
Ratio of agricultural workforce to total workforce	Waf	22.1	22.5
Volume of wage arrears by number of workers by average income in 1997	Dew97	1.69	1.0

Source: Survey 2000, Comittee for State Statistics of the Irkutsk Oblast, 1997, 2000; author's own calculations

Table 4-4 a: Estimation Results; Dependent Variable: Year when First Bakery Emerged; Model: Ordered Probit

Variables	Model 1	Model2	Model3
Regressors			Coefficient
Pop96	-.0023665	-.0034795*	-.0026198
In95	.0021699*	.0011257	.0026024*
Gra95		-.000029*	-.000043*
Dew97		.4369637*	.521098*
Wfa		-.055378	-.0246576*
Rub (1 = urban)			-2.241853*
Observations	35		31
Pseudo R squared	0.0539	0.1098	.1812

*significant at 5% level

Source: Survey 2000, Committee for State Statistics of the Irkutsk Oblast, 1997, 2000; author's own calculations

Table 4-4 b: Marginal Effects; Dependent Variable: Year when First Bakery Emerged; Model: Ordered Probit

Variable Model 1	Pop 96	Inc95	Gra95	Dew97	Wfa	Rub
Model 1						
First, rank=0	.0003875	-.0003553				
	(.00033)	(.00018)				
First, rank=1	.0004724	-.0004331				
	(.0004)	(.00023)				
First, rank=2	.0000655	-.0000601				
	(.00013)	(.00011)				
First, rank=3	-.0002387	.0002188				
	(.00022)	(.00014)				
First, rank=4	-.000123	.0001128				
	(.00013)	(.00009)				
First, rank=5	-.0000778	.0000713				
	(.0001)	(.00008)				
First, rank=11	-.0004859	.0004455				
	(.0004)	(.00021)				
Model 2						
First, rank=0	.0003709	-.00012	3.09e-06	-.0465751	.0005903	
	(.00029)	(.00014)	(.00000)	(.03424)	(.00136)	
First, rank=1	.0008302	-.0002686	6.92e-06	-.1042563	.0013213	
	(.00053)	(.00029)	(.00000)	(.06541)	(.00293)	
First, rank=2	.0001708	-.0000553	1.42e-06	-.021453	.0002719	
	(.00023)	(.00009)	(.00000)	(.02828)	(.00069)	
First, rank=3	-.0004385	.0001419	-3.66e-06	.055069	-.0006979	
	(.00034)	(.00016)	(.00000)	(.04203)	(.00158)	
First, rank=4	-.000248	.0000802	-2.07e-06	.0311461	-.0003947	
	(.00022)	(.0001)	(.00000)	(.02709)	(.00092)	
First, rank=5	-.000148	.0000479	-1.23e-06	.0185847	-.0002355	
	(.00017)	(.00007)	(.00000)	(.02014)	(.00058)	
First, rank=11	-.0005374	.0001739	-4.48e-06	.0674846	-.0008553	
	(.00036)	(.00019)	(.00000)	(.04393)	(.00191)	
Model 3						
First, rank=0	.0001886	-.0001873	3.10e-06	-.037509	.0017749	.3389341
	(.0002)	(.00016)	(.00000)	(.03048)	(.00164)	(.22028)
First, rank=1	.0006764	-.0006719	.0000111	-.1345317	.0063658	.3789489
	(.00055)	(.00039)	(.00001)	(.07229)	(.00402)	(.14135)
First, rank=2	.0001674	-.0001663	2.75e-06	-.0333066	.001576	-.0338487
	(.00022)	(.00019)	(.00000)	(.03808)	(.0019)	(.0861)
First, rank=3	-.0003961	.0003934	-6.50e-06	.0787778	-.0037277	-.2708616
	(.00036)	(.00028)	(.00000)	(.05438)	(.00279)	(.10485)
First, rank=4	-.0002225	.0002211	-3.65e-06	.0442655	-.0020946	-.1299073
	(.00023)	(.00018)	(.00000)	(.0357)	(.00188)	(.08863)
First, rank=5	-.0001249	.0001241	-2.05e-06	.0248435	-.0011756	-.0749186
	(.00015)	(.00013)	(.00000)	(.02568)	(.00133)	(.07325)
First, rank=11	-.0002889	.000287	-4.74e-06	.0574604	-.0027189	-.2083468
	(.00026)	(.00021)	(.00000)	(.03876)	(.00211)	(.1224)

Source: Survey 2000, Committee for State Statistics of the Irkutsk Oblast, 1997, 2000; author's own calculations

Table 4-4 shows the regression results. All variables except for population reveal some influence on the year the first bakery emerged in the district or town. However, the direction of the coefficients is not as expected in all cases and requires further discussion.

Out of the variables representing the market driven process, the population reveals the expected direction of coefficient but is not shown as significant. This is surprising as the emergence of new enterprises can be expected to be in compliance with demand. This hints towards a distortion of this relation. Furthermore, the income variable is positive which is not the result that was expected in the above discussion. Still this result is a hint that the transition process has started earlier in regions with lower average incomes which could be agricultural areas. This outcome is in compliance with the discussions in chapter three.

The results for the variables representing the transition process are as expected for the area under grain production and the ratio of agricultural workforce. The higher grain production in the region and the higher the share of agricultural workforce the more likely is the emergence of a bakery at an early stage. This is supported by the coefficient of the rural-urban dummy. An early emergence of bakeries is more likely in rural areas which supports the hypotheses set out in chapter three. The wage arrears became more relevant at a later stage in the transition process and explain the emergence of bakeries at a later stage.

4.4.3 Estimation Based on Production Units

It was mentioned above that the estimation based on spatial units might show weak results due to a small sample size. To support the results of the estimations based on spatial units in the following the larger sample of new bakeries will be used. In this case the year of emergence of the bakery will serve as the dependent variable. The ordered probit model as defined above applies. As the regressors in the case of single units can be chosen more precisely they will be grouped into variables representing the market driven process, the transition driven process, particularly representing the diffusion or distance approach and the old production system. The explanation for the choice of variables is given below:

Market Mechanism

- Population (*Pop96*): see above
- Average income per household in the region (*Inc95*): see above
- ***Distance to next bakery in the year of foundation***: This distance variable also represents demand, as provision with bread can be expected to be worse

and opening a bakery can be expected to be more profitable with increasing distance to the next bakery. Hence, the coefficient is expected to be negative (*Nextbak*).

Transition Mechanism

- Area under grain production in the district (*Gra95*): see above
- Wage arrears by number of workforce by average income in the district (*Dew97*): see above
- Ratio of agricultural workforce to total workforce in the district (*Waf*): see above
- ***Judicial form of the enterprise*** (*Org*): This variable cannot clearly be assigned to market mechanism or transition mechanism. This variable introduces a dummy that distinguishes between small businesses (org=1) and all other judicial forms (org=0). However, as the process is expected to start in rural areas the coefficient is expected to be positive, i.e. all other forms than small business are likely to emerge earlier.

Diffusion Mechanism

- **Distance to next town** (Nexttow): see below
- **Distance to Irkutsk** (Disirk): Distance to next town and distance to Irkutsk represent the market driven diffusion process or learning aspect of the emergence of new bakeries. As stated in section 4.2 the information about running businesses-undertakings starts in large centres, spreads to smaller centres and finally to more remote areas. Consequently, both coefficients are expected to be negative.

Old production system

- ***Presence of an old enterprise in the municipality*** (*Oldent*): If there exists already an enterprise at a certain location, new bakeries are expected to emerge at a later stage in the diffusion process.

The estimation shows that only three variables are significant, i.e. population, distance to the next bakery and the judicial form of the enterprise. The results show that bakeries that are located in districts with more population are likely to have started their business at an early stage. This partly contradicts the predictions in the theoretical part as it was expected that the diffusion starts in agricultural areas where generally the population is less. The other two variables support the expectations. In locations where the next bakery is far away, bakeries tend to have opened at an early stage. Furthermore, the positive sign of the coefficient for the judicial form of the enterprise shows that small businesses tend to have opened at a later stage.

Table 4-5: Summary Statistics; Dependent Variable: Year when First Bakery Emerged (first); Model: Ordered Probit

Regressor	Name	Mean	Standard deviation
Year when the first bakery emerged	First	4.48	2.06
Regressands			
Population at 01.01.1996	Pop96	67.98	108.61
Average monthly income per houshold in Roubles	In95	615.4	256.4
Distance to next bakery at year of foundation in km	Nextbak	3.8	13.1
Area under grain production in 1995	Gra95	25822.1	21760.9
Wage arrears by number of workforce by average income in the district	Dew97	1.8	1.0
Ratio of agricultural workforce to total workforce	Waf	22.7	22.7
Distance to next town in km	Nexttow	11.6	33.7
Distance to Irkutsk in km	Disirk	203.2	277.3

Source: Survey 2000, Committee for State Statistics of the Irkutsk Oblast, 1997, 2000; author's own calculations

Table 4-6 a: Estimation Results; Dependent Variable: Year when First Bakery Emerged (first); Model: Ordered Probit

Variable	Coefficient
Pop 96	-2.04e-06*
Inc95	-.0001838
Nextbak	-.0091173*
Org	.5361094*
Gra95	-4.18e-07
Dew97	.0256852
Waf	.0031954
Nexttow	-.0022176
Disirk	.000493
Oldent	.1846604

**significant on 5% level*

Source: Survey 2000, Committee for State Statistics of the Irkutsk Oblast, 1997, 2000; author's own calculations

Table 4-6 b: Marginal Effects; Dependent Variable: Year when First Bakery Emerged (first); Model: Ordered Probit

		Pop96	Inc95	Nextbak	Org	Gra95
First	rank=0	6.31E-08	-5.96E-06	0.0003337	-0.016968	-4.55E-08
		(0.00)	(0.00002)	(0.00026	(0.01282)	(0)
First	rank=1	2.16E-07	-0.0000204	0.001143	-0.054309	-1.56E-07
		(0.00)	(0.00006)	(0.00067	(0.03065)	(0)
First	rank=2	2.72E-07	-0.0000257	0.0014372	-0.065495	-1.96E-07
		(0.00)	(0.00008)	(0.00082	(0.0339)	(0)
First	rank=3	2.42E-07	-0.0000228	0.0012794	-0.056285	-1.75E-07
		(0.00)	(0.00007)	(0.00075	(0.02807)	0)
First	rank=4	9.65E-08	-9.12E-06	0.0005106	-0.021091	-6.97E-08
		(0.00)	(0.00003)	(0.00034	(0.01197)	((0)
First	rank=5	-5.61E-08	5.30E-06	-0.0002966	0.015122	4.05E-08
		(0.00)	(0.00002)	(0.00025	(0.01151)	(0)
First	rank=6	-2.69E-07	0.0000254	-0.0014238	0.0646808	1.94E-07
		(0.00)	(0.00008)	(0.00082	(0.03301)	(0)
First	rank=7	-3.12E-07	0.0000295	-0.0016498	0.0739155	2.25E-07
		(0.00)	(0.00009)	(0.00094	(0.03731)	(0)
First	rank=8	-2.52E-07	0.0000238	-0.0013337	0.0604291	1.82E-07
		(0.00)	(0.00007)	(0.00077	(0.0321)	(0)
		Dew97	Wfa	Disnext	Disirk	Oldent
First	rank=0	0.0001101	-0.0000278	-0.0000493	-1.48E-05	-0.0053066
		(0.00269)	(0.00019)	(0.00008	(0.00002)	(0.0077)
First	rank=1	0.0003772	-0.0000953	-0.0001687	-5.06E-05	-0.0184165
		(0.00923)	(0.00063)	(0.00026	(0.00005)	(0.02533)
First	rank=2	0.0004742	-0.0001198	-0.0002121	-6.36E-05	-0.023473
		(0.01161)	(0.0008)	(0.00033	(0.00006)	(0.03261)
First	rank=3	0.0004222	-0.0001067	-0.0001889	-5.66E-05	-0.0212874
		(0.01033)	(0.00071)	(0.00029	(0.00005)	(0.03025)
First	rank=4	0.0001685	-0.0000426	-0.0000754	-2.26E-05	-0.0088984
		(0.00412)	(0.00028)	(0.00012	(0.00002)	(0.01339)
First	rank=5	-0.0000979	0.0000247	0.0000438	0.0000131	0.0042263
		(0.0024)	(0.00017)	(0.00007	(0.00001)	(0.00592)
First	rank=6	-0.0004698	0.0001187	0.0002102	0.000063	0.0230146
		(0.0115)	(0.00092)	(0.00033	(0.00006)	(0.03161)
First	rank=7	-0.0005444	0.0001375	0.0002435	0.000073	0.0273973
		(0.01333)	(0.00079)	(0.00038	(0.00007)	(0.03844)
First	rank=8	-0.0004401	0.0001112	0.0001969	0.000059	0.0227438
		(0.01077)	(0.00074)	(0.00031	(0.00005)	(0.03322)

Source: Survey 2000, Committee for State Statistics of the Irkutsk Oblast, 1997, 2000; author's own calculations

4.5 Concluding Summary

The aim of the chapter was on the one hand to describe the where and the when of the emergence of new bakeries in the Irkutsk Oblast during transition and to reveal the determining factors. The description of the reallocation process was based on considerations of diffusion theory. The comparison of the diffusion curve that was predicted according to theoretical considerations and the diffusion curve as observed in the Oblast showed that the model of two overlying diffusion mechanisms describes the reallocation process. Consequently, the question 'Where have markets developed and where have markets not developed?' is valid. It was shown that a market mechanism and a transition mechanism coexist.

The analysis of the determining factors support this result to a limited extent. Though the estimations have limitations due to data availability and sample size, the results show that market factors as well as transition factors influence the reallocation process. However, a role of distance to economic centres on the emergence of new bakeries, i.e. the spatial aspect of diffusion could not be proved. Therefore, it becomes clear that there is a sharp rural-urban distinction in market development. Demand determines reallocation but this process is disturbed by the transition phenomena mainly in rural areas.

5. The Enterprise Population

5.1 Introduction

The main focus of the previous chapter was the course of transition in the bakery sector. The question was addressed as to where and when new bakeries emerged and by which factors this can be explained. The determinants of the process already contain important information as they support the hypothesis of an influence of transition factors on reallocation and market development. However, characterizing enterprises as coined by transition or as market oriented as discussed in chapter three requires a more detailed description of the enterprise population. This is the aim of the present chapter.

As becomes clear from the discussion in chapter three a significant change in the enterprise population is expected where in the end old production units and newly emerged production facilities make up the enterprise population. The two groups of old and newly emerged enterprises represent two different dimensions in the transition debate. The group of old enterprises represents the privatization aspect of market development; the group of new enterprises the building of markets from below and the development of entrepreneurship.

The aspect of privatization has been broadly discussed from various perspectives, for example, the technique of privatization like mass privatization to outsiders or to insiders or sales, the political implications of privatization and the effects on reallocation and efficiency. In Russia a mass privatization concept to insiders was chosen in order to guarantee irreversibility and high speed of the privatization process[69]. However, though a high speed in privatization was reached, other goals were missed. Regularly, core investors and insiders gained a major share which prevented restructuring and fostered the asset-stripping of enterprises. The same occurred in the food processing industry though a special approach was chosen for this industry. Because government saw a monopsonistic position of food processors towards agricultural producers and, consequently, a disadvantageous input-output-price relation, it was planned to give shares in food processing enterprises to agricultural producers. However, as the law was launched most of the enterprises were already privatized[70]. As a result of the pri-

69 Roland, 2000, p. 21, pp. 87 ff., pp. 229 ff.
70 Wandel in Wehrheim et al., 2000, p. 368.

vatization process, restructuring and adjustments in the location of old enterprises were severely hampered.

As shown in the preceding chapter, new entrepreneurs play a crucial role in the new spatial organization of the industry. However, they have found less attention in the literature. Small- and medium- scale enterprises (SME) play a significant role for job creation and innovation in most of the economies. This role is even strengthening over time. Still very little is known about new small-scale enterprises in Russia although their significance is widely noticed. The topics mainly discussed in this regard are the informal financial obstacles to entrepreneurship. Most of the survey results presented in publications are references to these questions[71]. Again the analysis of the enterprises of a single industry has been neglected. The present chapter will help to fill this gap.

A study by Earle & Sakova (1999) on the entry decision into self-employment in six different transition countries excludes agricultural activities because agricultural entrepreneurship is partly seen as subsistence, and therefore not regarded as entrepreneurship. Bakeries are of a hybrid nature in this regard. On the level of a single entrepreneur, bakeries are clearly a small-business-undertaking. However, as discussed in chapter three, on the level of agricultural enterprises or former kolchozes a kind of subsistence production with division of labor on the kolchoz level can prevail and might include bread baking. To distinguish between these two groups of enterprises is the task of the present chapter.

The ideas of chapter three result in an enterprise population that can be divided into four groups. The descriptions of the groups finish with a statement on the market orientation of each group. This will be the criterion that leads through the study of the enterprise population.

First the grouping of the enterprises will be explained. While the old enterprises will be treated as one group in the following descriptions, the new enterprises are subgrouped by means of cluster analysis. The chapter will conclude with a summary of the results stressing the market orientation of enterprises as an expression of transition distortions or market development.

5.2 Grouping of the Enterprise Population

The enterprise population in the regions of the Irkutsk Oblast covered by the survey in the year 2000 consists of 261 bread production facilities. The number of plants is taken from official statistics and information provided by Business Karta

71 Chepurenko, 1998; Audretsch, 1994; Julien, 1993; Schwalbach, 1994; Applegate, 1994; Levitsky, 1996; OECD, 1999.

while the number of old units belonging to the additional system and the number of new units stem from observations of the survey[72].

Table 5-1: Number of Bread Production Units in the Irkutsk Oblast in 2000

Old		New	Total
Plants	Additional system	Bakeries	
17	32	212	261

Source: Committee for State Statistics in the Irkutsk Oblast, 1999, p.5, Business Karta 1999.

As the aim is to distinguish between market oriented and non-market oriented enterprises a method must be found to classify the production units according to this criterion. Basically two approaches are possible: to find a method that divides the total population into groups in an explorative manner or to define groups beforehand on theoretical grounds and assign the enterprises to the groups. In a situation where little is known about the structure of the enterprise population, as holds for the new enterprises in the present context, the second approach does not appeal because it fixes the groups and is not open to the formation of groups that were not expected beforehand. Consequently, for the present study an explorative approach is chosen although an idea of the grouping exists.

The traditional methodology for classification is cluster analysis. It is highly explorative in nature as the results can vary widely depending on the choice of proximity/distance measures, cluster algorithms and variables. For these reasons it is necessary to base the analysis on some theoretical consideration. The discussion of chapter three results in three groups of new enterprises out of which two are characterized as non-market-oriented small businesses and one is characterized as a market-oriented small business. Hence a grouping of two or three is expected.

5.2.1 Choice of Variables

For the cluster analysis variables were chosen that represent the market orientation of the enterprises while general criteria like size etc. were neglected for different reasons. On the one hand the description should reveal whether there are significant differences in the groups regarding size, assortment, cost structure and

72 See chapter four.

the like; on the other hand, can additional variables blur the differences between the groups if they do not fully represent the idea behind the classification[73].

Legal form of the enterprise: The choice of this variable is based on the assumption that bakeries in such an early stage of market development belong to small businesses and can hardly take the form of a joint stock company for example. These are agricultural or industrial enterprises that operate a bakery. As to the question of the legal form of the enterprises, six different answers were possible as given in table 5-2. Cluster analysis requires a binary code for nominal data. For this reason, it became necessary to recode the six categories into two categories. According to the assumption made above, small business was coded as one and all other legal forms as zero. Though bakeries could possibly be limited liability companies, this form was assigned zero as well. The frequencies for the legal form of enterprises are represented in table 5-2.

Table 5-2: Legal Form of the New Bread Producing Units in the Irkutsk Oblast in 2000

	Frequency	Per cent
State enterprise	18	8.5
Municipal enterprise	3	1.4
Joint stock company, closed type	28	13.2
Joint stock company, open type	28	13.2
Private limited company	26	12.3
Co-operative	25	11.8
Small business	80	37.7
Others	4	1.9
Total	212	100.0

Source: Survey 2000

Influence of competitor prices on price formation[74]: This variable was included because it is expected that enterprises that can be characterized as subsistence production price bread for the workers of their enterprise based merely on costs, while enterprises that appear in competitive markets have to take competitor prices into account. However, the price formation of businesses in a monopoly market blurs the distinction. The question of the influence of competitor prices on price formation could be answered on a five-point scale with one for no influence and five for high influence. Again, the data had to be recoded into a binary variable. If the answer was one or two for no or little influence the variable

73 Backhaus et al., 1994, pp. 260 ff.; Eckes & Rossbach, 1980; Everitt, 1993.

74 For the precise question see the questionnaire in the appendix.

was coded zero, while for three to five it was coded one. The distribution of answers to this question is shown in table 5-3.

Table 5-3: Influence of Competitor Prices on Price Formation of New Bread Producing Units in the Irkutsk Oblast in 2000

		Frequency	Per cent
Valid	Not important	110	57.3
	2.00	10	5.2
	3.00	16	8.3
	4.00	22	11.5
	Most important	34	17.7
	Total	192	100.0
Missing	System	20	
Total		212	

Source: Survey 2000

Source of raw materials: The source of raw materials represents the aspect of vertical integration occurring during transition. If there is vertical integration, i.e. the enterprise uses its own grain, transition distortions are assumed and the variable is coded zero. If only bought inputs are used the enterprise is assumed to be market-oriented and the variable is coded one. Enterprises were supposed to give the percentage of the different possible sources of raw materials in their sourcing. Hence, a production unit could answer that it used only its own grain, only bought grain and flour or a combination of both. The frequencies of the binary variable, which is coded zero for use of own grain and one for no use of own grain are given in table 5-4.

Table 5-4: Use of Own Grain for Bread Production of the New Bread Producing Units in the Irkutsk Oblast in 2000

		Frequency	Per cent
Valid	No	120	57.7
	Yes	88	42.3
	Total	208	100.0
Missing	System	4	
Total		212	

Source: Survey 2000

Use of barter in transactions: Comparable to the source of raw materials, the barter criterion represents distortions that have emerged during the transition process. The enterprises were asked for the share of barter in purchasing different inputs and for the share of barter on the marketing side as well. Though the share of barter is very low compared to other sectors of the economy, it is still a relevant variable. Code 1 was assigned for no barter and zero for the use of barter irrespective of the kind of transaction. The frequencies are given in table 5-5.

Table 5-5: The Role of Barter in the Transactions of New Bread Producing Units in the Irkutsk Oblast in 2000

		Frequency	Valid per cent
Valid	No barter	105	51.0
	Use of barter	101	49.0
	Total	206	100.0
Missing	System	6	
Total		212	

Source: Survey 2000

Competition from local enterprises: The enterprises were asked to assess the importance of competition from local enterprises on a five-point scale. The coding of the variable is identical to the variable of influence of competitor prices on price formation and the results are shown in table 5-6.

Table 5-6: The Role of Competition of Local Enterprises for the New Bread Producing Units in the Irkutsk Oblast in 2000

		Frequency	Valid per cent
Valid	No competition	64	31.4
	2.00	14	6.9
	3.00	35	17.2
	4.00	10	4.9
	High competition	81	39.7
	Total	204	100.0
Missing	System	8	
Total		212	

Source: Survey 2000

For the classification other variations of variables were employed but did not produce a clearer distinction of groups. Furthermore, additional variables lead to an increase in missing observations. For the sake of a clear distinction between the groups and a higher number of observations included in the classification the five variables described above were chosen.

5.2.2 Choice of Measures

Various combinations of proximity/distance measures and clustering algorithms were employed. None of the combinations produced more than three groups with a reasonable number of members in the group. Several combinations produced two or three groups. However, none of the classifications with three groups delivered results that could be interpreted in a meaningful way. Hence, a classification of two groups remains. The sizes of the groups produced by different combinations of algorithms differed but not significantly. However, one strength of the groups was repeated by several combinations of measure and algorithm that at the same time delivers the sharpest distinction between the groups. Hence, using a Rogers and Tanimoto distance measure and a within-group-linkage-algorithm for the five variables mentioned above, the following groups of observations are gained.

5.2.3 Description of the Clusters

Cluster one contains 116 enterprises (63 per cent; N=183) while cluster two contains 67 enterprises (37 per cent). According to the statistics of the variables used for the cluster analysis for each cluster, cluster one can be characterized as ***market oriented*** and cluster two as ***non-market oriented***. The statistics are given in table 5-7.

Almost all enterprises of the legal form 'small business' are included in the market oriented cluster with an exception of 4 units (5 per cent). They amount up to 57.8 per cent of the units in the market oriented cluster. The largest group of the remaining 43 per cent is private limited companies (15.5 per cent) which is in compliance with the expectations. Furthermore, this is supported by the distribution of legal forms in the non-market oriented cluster. Joint stock companies, both closed and open types (23.9 per cent and 26.9 per cent respectively) and cooperatives (25.4 per cent) make up 76.2 per cent of the enterprises in the non-market oriented cluster, while private limited companies and small businesses are of little importance (six per cent in either case). However, the share of enterprises in the market oriented cluster that have legal forms other than small business, like state enterprise and joint stock company, is relatively high (26.7 per cent) and does not fit into the picture. It serves as an indicator that a group of enterprises exist which operate bakeries not entirely as part of the virtual economy but as a market-oriented business. This again is in compliance with the expectation.

The results for the criterion of the influence of competitor prices on price formation show a very clear distinction between the groups. While in the non-market oriented cluster 91.0 per cent of the enterprises state that competitor prices do not have influence on their price formation, the distribution of answers in the market oriented cluster shows a two piece pattern. 37.9 per cent of units state that competitor prices are not important to their price formation while 27.6 per cent chose the highest importance and 15.5 per cent the second highest important influence of competitor prices on price formation. This supports the expectation that the structure of the markets in which the units are located divides the group. Market oriented bakeries in monopolies do not show an influence of competitor prices while enterprises in a competitive market do.

Less distinct is the distribution of the estimation of competition by local enterprises within the groups, though the generally expected picture remains. In the market oriented cluster only 10 per cent of the enterprises state that they do not experience competition while 60.3 per cent state very high competition. 19.0 per cent indicate three on the five-point-scale. In the non- market oriented cluster 68.7 per cent indicate no competition. However, 32 per cent remain that state some form of competition, which is not expected in this group. This again hints at the existence of a third group of new enterprises.

Again, the results are very clear for the criterion source of inputs. Looking at the distribution for bought flour, 80.2 per cent of the market oriented cluster answer that they use bought flour at 100 per cent, while 91 per cent of the units in the non- market oriented cluster do not use bought flour at all. The units in this cluster that use their own grain to 100 per cent is up to 88.1 per cent.

As distinct is the use of barter between the groups. Given the relatively low share of barter in industries for consumer goods, high shares of use of barter cannot be expected. The most relevant type of barter transactions in the given context is payment in kind for workers and should serve as a representative of the use of barter. However, 80.5 per cent of the units in the market oriented cluster say they do not use barter at all, while 37.9 per cent of the units in the market oriented cluster say they pay their workers in kind. This is very much in compliance with the expectation of the behavior of market-oriented and non-market oriented enterprises.

The description of the different criteria used for the cluster analysis within the groups shows clearly that the distinction between market oriented and non-market oriented enterprises is very relevant. Though the distinction is not perfectly clear in all variables used, the two-group picture remains. Consequently, this grouping will be kept for the following description of the enterprise population. Moreover, it has to be noted that the hypothesized third group, as discussed in chapter 3.5.2, was not identified by the cluster analysis. However, it does not mean that the group does not exist. It is possible that the variables used do not suffice to distinguish the third group or the group is too small to be clearly distinguished.

Table 5-7: Statistics of Variables Used in Cluster Analysis According to the Resulting Clusters

	Market oriented cluster		Non-market oriented cluster	
Number of observations	116		67	
Legal form of the enterprise				
	Number	Percentage	Number	Percentage
State enterprise	8	6,9	6	9,0
Municipal enterprise	13	2,6		0,0
Joint stock company, closed type	10	8,6	16	23,9
Joint stock company, open type	5	4,3	18	26,9
Private limited company	18	15,5	4	6,0
Co-operative	4	3,4	17	25,4
Small business	67	57,8	4	6,0
Others	1	0,9	2	3,0
Influence of competitor prices on price formation				
	Number	Percentage	Number	Percentage
1 Not important	44	37,9	61	91,0
2	8	6,9	2	3,0
3	14	12,1	1	1,5
4	18	15,5	2	3,0
5 Very important	32	27,6	1	1,5
Competition by local enterprises				
	Number	Percentage	Number	Percentage
1 No competition	12	10,3	46	68,7
2	4	3,4	6	9,0
3	22	19,0	10	14,9
4	8	6,9	1	1,5
5 High competition	70	60,3	4	6,0
Source of raw material in %				
Bought grain, externally milled	Number	Percentage	Number	Percentage
0	106	91,4	67	100
1-99	2	1,8	0	0
100	8	6,9	0	0

	Market oriented cluster		Non-market oriented cluster	
Number of observations	116		67	
Bought grain, own mill				
0	108	93,1	65	97
1-99	2	1,8	2	3
100	6	5,2		
Bought flour				
0	18	15,5	61	91
1-99	5	4,3	3	7,5
100	92	80,2	1	1,5
Own grain, externally milled				
0	115	99,1	45	67,2
1-99	1	0,9	3	4,5
100	0	0	19	28,4
Own grain, own mill				
0	110	94,8	23	34,3
1-99	4	3,5	4	6
100	2	1,7	40	59,7
Payment in kind with workers				
	Number	Percentage	Number	Percentage
No barter	91	80,5	25	37,9
1-10%	6	5,3	8	12,1
11-20%	6	5,3	9	13,6
21-30%	2	1,8	4	6,1
31-40%	0	0	0	0
41-50%	2	1,8	5	7,6
51-60%	2	1,8	0	0
61-70%	0	0	1	1,5
71-80%	1	0,9	2	3,0
81-90%	2	1,8	1	1,5
91-100%	1	0,9	11	16,7

Source: Survey 2000; author's own calculations

5.3 Description of the Enterprise Population

The explanation of the grouping procedure and the resulting clusters showed the relevance of the idea of market orientation in the development of new enterprises in the bread industry of the Irkutsk Oblast. However, due to reasons of sharpness in the groupings and of feasibility only a selected number of variables were included and described. If the distinction between market oriented and non-market oriented units is relevant, it should be reflected in other criteria, also. Furthermore, the market orientation of the already existing units has to be assessed and compared to the figures for the new enterprises. Therefore, the description of the enterprise population in the following paragraphs will continue the idea of market orientation in the interpretation and will have to repeat the expressions of some of the variables explained above in order to integrate the old production units. The idea of market development that is distorted by transition phenomena should reveal differences in the groups in almost all possible criteria, be they directly related to transition phenomena like reasons to establish a bakery or of a more general nature like size of the production units or assortment.

5.3.1 Position in the Course of Transition

Variables that reflect the discussion in the preceding chapter are the date of foundation, the reasons for establishing a bakery, and the rural-urban distinction in the location of enterprises. According to the discussions in the preceding chapter the two clusters should show the following differences: The diffusion process was assumed to start earlier and go faster in the rural areas as these enterprises have to react to an economic situation and the diffusion cannot be put down to a learning process. Hence, the enterprises in the non-market oriented cluster are expected to be located in rural areas and to be founded earlier than the enterprises in the market oriented cluster. Furthermore, the enterprises in the market oriented cluster should be located in urban areas as well as in rural areas.

The results of both criteria as shown in tables 5-8 and 5-10 confirm the expectation. The rural-urban distribution is very distinct, where 92.5 per cent of the enterprises in the non-market oriented cluster are located in rural areas while 63 per cent of the enterprises in the market oriented cluster are located in urban areas and 37 per cent in rural areas. Less sharp, but still in accordance with the expectation, is the course of foundations within the groups. The process starts a year earlier in the non-market oriented cluster. However, unexpectedly, the course is comparable to the normal diffusion process and does not proceed faster than in the market oriented cluster. The course in the market oriented cluster is also comparable to the normal diffusion process, though the peak in 1998 is enormous. This could be due to missing observations in the cluster analysis. However, the comparison of the means is significant.

Table 5-8: Date of Foundation of New Bread Producing Units in the Irkutsk Oblast in 2000 According to the Clusters

Year	Market oriented cluster		Non-market oriented cluster	
	Number	Percentage	Number	Percentage
1992	0	0	4	6
1993	5	4.3	7	10.4
1994	13	11.2	9	13.4
1995	17	14.7	11	16.4
1996	14	12.1	11	16.4
1997	14	12.1	13	19.4
1998	30	25.9	4	6.0
1999	14	12.1	5	7.5
2000	9	7.8	3	4.5
Means	1996.81		1995.73	

Source: Survey 2000

Table 5-9: Independent Samples Test for the Date of Foundation of New Bread Producing Units in the Irkutsk Oblast in 2000.

	t-test for equality of means				
	t	df	Sig. (2-tailed)	Mean difference	Std. error difference
Equal variances assumed	3.494	181	.001	1.08	.31
Equal variances not assumed	3.430	130.192	.001	1.08	.31

Source: Survey 2000; author's own calculations

Table 5-10: Rural-urban Distribution of the New Bread Producing Units in the Irkutsk Oblast in 2000 According to the Clusters

			Frequency	Valid per cent
Market oriented cluster	Valid	Rural	42	36.5
		Urban	73	63.5
		Total	115	100.0
	Missing	System	1	
	Total		116	
Non-market oriented cluster	Valid	Rural	62	92.5
		Urban	5	7.5
		Total	67	100.0

Source: Survey 2000

Table 5-11: The Reasons for Establishing a Bakery for the New Bread Producing Enterprises in the Irkutsk Oblast in 2000 According to the Clusters

	Market oriented cluster			Non-market oriented cluster		
	Count	% of responses	% of cases	Count	% of responses	% of cases
On the base of an old enterprise	13	8.7	12.1	3	3.4	4.6
To provide the workers of the main enterprise with bread	9	6.0	8.4	25	28.4	**38.5**
To provide the population with bread	23	15.3	**21.5**	24	27.3	**36.9**
Integration on the raw material side	4	2.7	3.7	10	11.4	15.4
Integration on the marketing side	8	5.3	7.5			
It is a profitable business	42	28.0	**39.3**	7	8.0	10.8
Old supply system broke down, no other bakery	13	8.7	12.1	12	13.6	**18.5**
To provide higher quality	4	2.7	3.7	1	1.1	1.5
To create jobs	14	9.3	13.1	1	1.1	1.5
Others	20	13.4	**18.7**	5	5.6	7.7
Valid cases	107			65		
Missing cases	9			2		

Source: Survey 2000

The reasons for establishing a bakery were asked for in an open question. The answers should reflect the market orientation or the survival orientation of the enterprises. Taken the percentage of cases, a comparison of the three most important answers between the groups shows that this criterion also approves the expected distinction between the enterprises. The three most frequently named reasons given by enterprises in the market oriented cluster are 'To provide the population with bread', 'It is a profitable business' and 'To create jobs', while the three most important answers given by enterprises in the non-market oriented cluster are 'To provide workers of the main enterprise with bread', 'To provide the population with bread', 'The old supply system broke down'. While 'It is a profitable business' has a much lower share in the non-market oriented cluster, the answer 'To provide the workers of the main enterprise with bread' is negligible in the market oriented cluster. That the answer 'To provide the population with bread' appears in both clusters as important can be explained by a peculiarity in the Russian/Soviet language. The Russian term for population leaves open whether the population of the main enterprise is meant, as the former agricultural units also represented a society, or whether the population independent of the agricultural enterprise is meant.

5.3.2 Behavior on Markets and the Role of Prices

Hand in hand with the characterization of the enterprises goes their behavior on markets. Enterprises which operate a bakery with the purpose of providing their own workers with bread should reveal less influence of impulses from the market on their behavior. The criteria to check for this assumption are the role of demand and of competitors. In the case of enterprises producing for their workers a pure cost pricing can be assumed while other enterprises are expected to show effects of demand and of competitors on their behavior. Furthermore, these criteria should shed light on the situation of the old enterprises. Hence, table 5-12 shows the results of all groups of enterprises, the two groups of new enterprises, the old plants and the enterprises that formerly belonged to the additional system in rural areas. Unfortunately, out of 17 old plants counted in the preceding chapter, survey data is available only for ten.

The answers about the role of prices of raw materials on price formation is 'most important' for all groups involved as can be expected and there are hardly any differences between the groups. Differences emerge with the questions about the role of demand and competitor prices on price formation where the answers prove the degree of involvement in markets. The old bread plants show the strongest influence of demand and competitor prices, which supports the discussion in chapter three. The old bread plants have lost part of their markets and at the same time try to run their capacities. In contrast to these are the answers of the enterprises of the market oriented cluster and the additional system. In both groups enterprises clearly exist which show no influence of competitor prices, which indicates enterprises in a monopoly position. The remainder of the two groups is not clearly distinguished. While in the case of demand the share of enterprises which answer that demand has an impact to a medium degree on their price formation and the percentage of enterprises who indicate a very high influence is 16 per cent and 12 per cent respectively, the answers in the case of competitor prices reveal a clear distinction in the case of the market oriented cluster of the new enterprises. 27 per cent indicate a very strong influence of competitor prices on price formation. The enterprises of the additional system seem to be under much less pressure for adjustment which can be explained by their

Table 5-12: Factors Influencing Price Formation and the Role of Competitors for the Bread Producing Enterprises in the Irkutsk Oblast in 2000.

	Market oriented cluster		Non-market oriented cluster		Old plants		Additional system	
	Number	%	Number	%	Number	%	Number	%
Influence of prices for raw materials on price formation								
Not important	1	0.9	4	6.0	0	0	2	6.3
2	1	0.9	2	3.0	0	0	0	0
3	3	2.6	8	11.9	0	0	1	3.1
4	4	3.5	4	6.0	1	10	3	9.4
Very important	106	92.2	49	73.1	9	90	26	81.3
Total	115		67		10		32	
Missing	1		0					
Influence of demand on price formation								
Not important	44	40.7	47	70.1	0	0	19	59.4
2	12	11.1	5	7.5	1	10	2	6.3
3	21	19.4	5	7.5	3	30	5	15.6
4	13	12.0	4	6.0	3	30	2	6.3
Very important	18	16.7	5	7.5	3	30	4	12.5
Mean	2.52		1.71		3.8		2.06	
Total	108		66		10		32	
Missing	8		1					
Influence of competitor prices on price formation								
Not important	44	37.9	61	91.0	0	0	16	50.0
2	8	6.9	2	3.0	1	10	5	15.6
3	14	12.1	1	1.5	4	40	3	9.4
4	18	15.5	2	3.0	1	10	3	9.4
Very important	32	27.6	1	1.5	3	30	5	15.6
Mean	2.87		1.20		3.66		2.25	
Total	116		67		9		32	
Missing					1			
Competition by local enterprises								
Not important	12	10.3	46	68.7	0	0	11	34.4
2	4	3.4	6	9.0	2	20	2	6.3
3	22	19.0	10	14.9	0	0	6	18.8
4	8	6.9	1	1.5	0	0	4	12.5
Very important	70	60.3	4	6.0	8	80	9	28.1
Mean	4.03		1.67		4.4		2.93	
Total	116		67		10		32	

Source: Survey 2000

location in rural areas. The non-market oriented cluster of the new enterprises approves the little effect of market on their behavior: 70 per cent state that demand does not have an influence and 91 per cent that competitor prices do not have any influence on their price formation. The question about the experience of competition by local enterprises delivers the same picture with a much stronger emphasis on competition in the cases of the enterprises in the market oriented cluster and the old bread plants. Additionally, the old plants were asked for the significance of competition from old plants and from new bakeries. Out of eight enterprises that have answered six indicated high competition from small bakeries.

5.3.3 Sourcing and Marketing Channels

The sourcing and marketing relations of the enterprises are the criteria where the virtual economy finds its expression in a most distinct way with regard to the partners and the transactions with partners. Figure 5-1 shows the bread production units and their sourcing and marketing relations. The distinct role of the use of their own raw materials for the new bakeries, as discussed above, is repeated in the figure. The sourcing channels of the old bread plants indicate a diversification of the raw material sources. The picture indicates that the change in the partners for sourcing purposes for the old bread plants is significant. Seven out of ten enterprises source from a mix of agricultural enterprises, farmers, wholesale trade and flour processing plants, while three source from flour processing plants at 100 per cent. However, taking the share of each source in the total volume of purchases, the situation changes considerably. All enterprises that use a mix of different sources still purchase from flour processing plants at 90 per cent or more. Hence, the diversification of purchasing channels is limited and can be regarded as complementary to the traditional channel in the case of a lack of raw materials.

Clearly, the role of partners depends on the source of raw materials. For example, enterprises that use bought flour tend to source from the wholesale trade. Consequently, the picture for the non-market oriented cluster of new bakeries which use their own grain almost to 100 per cent mainly co-operate with mills, their own mills or other mills, while the commercial bakeries of the market oriented cluster have different partners out of which those most often indicated are mills (77.2 per cent) followed by wholesale trade (51.8 per cent) and middlemen (29.3 per cent) as shown in table 5-13 and 5-14.

The sourcing policy of bread production units of the former additional system in rural areas is unclear. 59.4 per cent use bought flour to 100 per cent, while 15.9 per cent use their own grain to 100 per cent, which is rather surprising. The most often named trading partners for them are mills and the wholesale trade.

Figure 5-1: Sourcing and Marketing Channels of Old Bread Plants and of New Bakeries in the Irkutsk Oblast in 2000

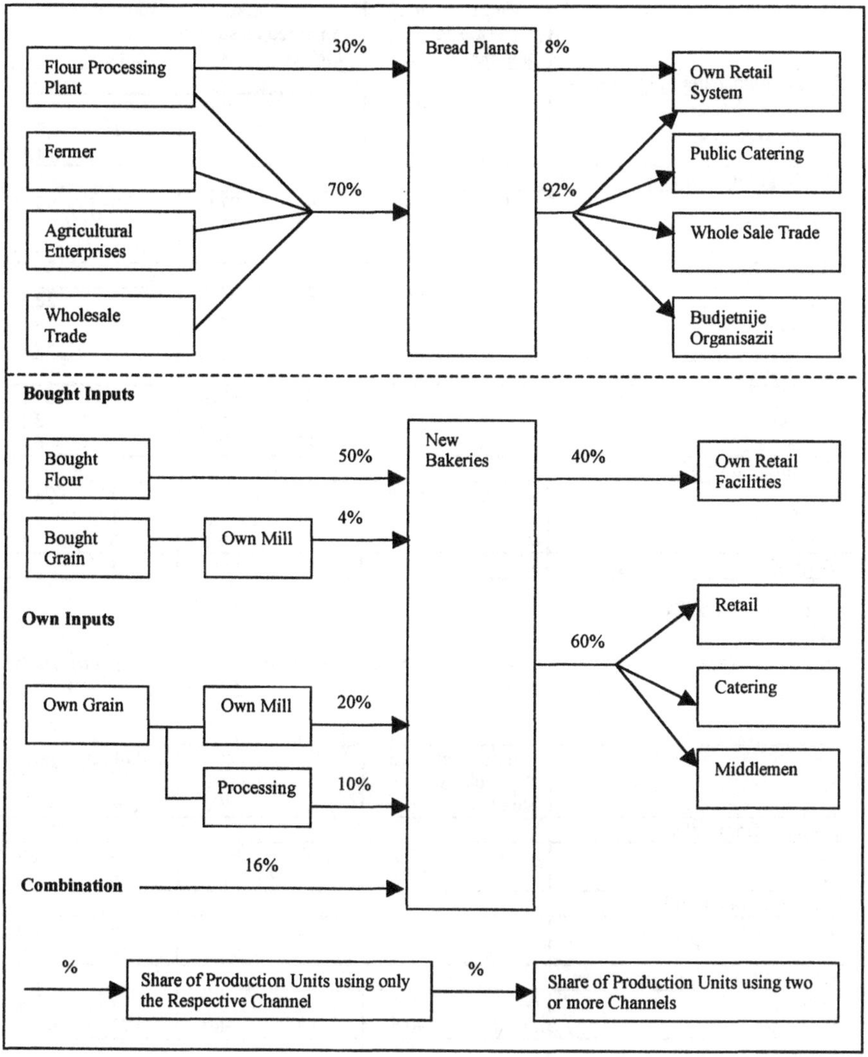

Source: author's own drawing

Table 5-13: Sources of Raw Materials for the New Enterprises of the Two Clusters and the Enterprises of the Additional System in the Irkutsk Oblast in 2000

	Market oriented cluster		Non-market oriented cluster		Additional system	
	Number	%	Number	%	Number	%
Bought grain, externally milled						
0 %	106	91.4	0	100	29	90.6
1-99 %	2	1.8			1	3.1
100 %	8	6.9			1	3.1
Bought grain, own mill						
0 %	108	93.1	65	97.0	30	93.8
1-99 %	2	1.8	2	3.0		
100 %	6	5.2			1	3.1
Bought flour						
0 %	18	15.5	61	91.0	9	28.1
1-99 %	5	4.3	5	7.5	3	9.3
100 %	93	80.2	1	1.5	19	59.4
Own grain, externally milled						
0 %	115	99.1	45	67.2	28	87.5
1-99 %	1	0.9	3	4.5	1	3.1
100 %	0	0	19	28.4	2	6.3
Own grain, own mill						
0 %	110	94.8	23	34.3	25	78.1
1-99 %	4	3.5	4	1.5	1	3.1
100 %	2	1.7	40	59.7	5	15.6
Missing					1	

Source: Survey 2000

Table 5-14: Partners of the New Bread Production Units of the Two Clusters and the Enterprises of the Additional System on the Sourcing Side in the Irkutsk Oblast in 2000.

	Market oriented cluster		Non-market oriented cluster		Additional system	
	Number	%	Number	%	Number	%
Sourcing from mills						
Yes	88	77.2	62	98.4	24	80
No	26	22.8	1	1.6	6	20
Sourcing from middlemen						
Yes	34	29.3	2	3.0	6	20
No	79	68.1	61	91.0	24	80
Sourcing from trade companies						
Yes	11	9.6	0	0	7	23.3
No	103	90.4	63	100	23	76.7
Mean (%)						
Sourcing from wholesale trade						
Yes	59	51.8	0	0	13	43.3
No	55	48.2	63	100	17	56.7
Missing	2	1.7	4	6.0	2	6.3

Source: Survey 2000

Though the relations of the old enterprises have changed only to a small extent regarding the kind of trading partners, the stability of links is not reflected in the duration of co-operation. Relations with partners that are older than ten years are of relevance for none of the groups. For all groups the relations are occasional or last since one to three years. Longer lasting relations play a less significant role (see table 5-15).

Table 5-15: Stability of Relations with Partners for the Bread Producing Units in the Irkutsk Oblast in 2000

	Market oriented cluster		Non-market oriented cluster		Additional system		Old plants	
	Number	%	Number	%	Number	%	Number	%
Share of transactions with occasional partners								
0 %	65	57.0	16	33.3	7	25.9	0	0
1-99 %	21	18.4	1	2.1	7	25.9	7	77.8
100%	28	24.6	31	64.6	13	48.1	1	11.1
Share of transactions with stable relations 1-3 years								
0 %	45	39.5	38	79.2	23	82.1	4	44.4
1-99 %	21	18.4	1	2.1	3	10.7	4	44.4
100%	48	42.1	9	18.8	2	7.1	1	11.1
Share of transactions with stable relations 3-5 years								
0 %	99	86.8	42	87.5	24	85.7	7	77.8
1-99 %	6	6.3			1	3.6	2	22.2
100%	9	7.9	6	12.5	3	10.7		
Share of transactions with stable relations 5-10 years								
0 %	109	95.6	47	97.9	26	92.9	7	77.8
1-99 %	1	0.9			1	3.6	1	11.1
100%	4	3.5	1	2.1	1	3.6	1	11.1
Share of transactions with stable relations more than 10 years								
0 %	113	99.1	48	100	24	88.9	6	66.7
1-99 %					3	11.1	2	22.2
100%	1	0.9					1	11.1
Missing	2	1.7	19	28.4	5	15.6	1	10

Source: Survey 2000

Regarding the marketing of the produce, not only are the partners and the relations with them of interest, but also the number of selling locations. It has been discussed in chapter three that in general the bread industry is composed of a large number of small local markets, where little interdependence through exchange is expected. On the other hand the peculiarities of the region, i.e. low population density and high number of small settlements, as well as the development in the transition environment, hint at the existence of deliveries of bread from the production location to other locations. Table 5-16 shows the number of enterprises selling at one or more locations and the respective average shares in the total sales. The table contains only the numbers for the new bakeries, because the old bread plants, as well as many of the small enterprises founded before 1992, serve the whole raion with their production, the former concentrated on urban areas, the latter on rural areas. Though in some districts the additional system completely broke down, which partly explains the emergence of new entities, in other districts the additional system still functions unchanged.

It can be stated that despite the regional peculiarities the rule of the local markets prevails. Though the number of enterprises that deliver bread to a second (52 per cent and 67 per cent) and third location (28 per cent and 11 per cent) is high, the average shares sold at the respective locations indicate that the significance is rather low. The share of enterprises in the non-market oriented cluster that deliver to other locations is higher for the second location and could be expected to be higher also for the third and fourth locations. This can be explained by the prevalence of the former kolkhoz system that comprised several villages. As a result, the agricultural enterprises maintain a central bakery and deliver further. However, the share of bread that is sold at other locations is lower for these companies than for the market oriented bakeries. It gives a slight hint to the argument of minimum scale for viability that is reached by delivering several locations discussed in chapter three. Nevertheless, the shares of total sales sold at the main location are high with 85.9 per cent and 89.9 per cent respectively.

Table 5-16: Share of Selling Locations of the New Bread Production Entities in the Irkutsk Oblast in Summer 2000

	Market oriented cluster			Non-market oriented cluster		
	Number	%	Share of location in total sales	Number	%	Share of location in total sales
Selling location 1	116	100	85.9	67	100	89.89
Selling location 2	56	48	20.24	27	67	23
Selling location 3	26	28	12.75	7	11	10
Selling location 4	13	12	11.25	4	6	10
Selling location 5	11	10	10	0	0	0

Source: Survey 2000

More distinct and in accordance with the interpretation of the clusters are the shares of different marketing channels in total sales as given in table 5-17. While for both clusters their own retail system is the most important marketing channel, its significance is much higher for the non-market oriented cluster in which enterprises sell on average 83 per cent through this channel. For the market oriented cluster the shares lie at 59 per cent and 27 per cent for other retail trade as the second most important retail channel. The enterprises of the additional system lie between the two clusters while the use of marketing channels of the old bread plants is most diverse. They deliver in equal shares through their own retail facilities and other retail facilities. Furthermore, their share of produce sold through middlemen is the highest with 17.50 per cent. While middlemen have some significance for the market oriented bakeries and the enterprises of the additional system (6.63 per cent and 8.83 per cent respectively), its significance for the enterprises of the non-market oriented cluster is negligible (1.76 per cent). In turn, the share of deliveries to public catering is higher (4.98 per cent) than for the other groups (around one per cent). The figures support the market orientation and non-market orientation of the clusters and a new orientation in marketing of the old bread plants.

Table 5-17: Share of Marketing Channels of the Bread Producing Units in the Irkutsk Oblast in Summer 2000

	Market oriented cluster		Non-market oriented cluster		Additional system		Old plants	
	N	% of total sales	N	% of total sales	N	% of total sales	N	% of total sales
Share of marketing through retail trade	109	27.73	65	6.01	30	16.06	8	35.13
Share of deliveries to public catering	109	0.92	65	4.98	30	1.28	8	1.11
Share of marketing through own retail facilities	109	59.03	65	83.35	31	71.67	8	35.75
Share of marketing to middlemen	109	6.63	65	1.76	31	8.38	8	17.50
Share of marketing through other channels	109	5.62	65	3.95	31	1.14	8	4.67

Source: Survey 2000

Another aspect is relevant in the description of the different marketing situations for the bread producing units. They can only sell production in locations to which they have access. This was the background to the question whether the enterprises have problems in selling at specific locations. Though entry barriers were not among the problems, the answers to the question underline the above argumentation. The enterprises of the non-market oriented cluster, which produce for their own use as expected, do not face any problems in selling their production; there is no competitor and as they to some extent pay their workers with bread they do not face demand problems like low purchasing power. The market oriented new bakeries and the old bread plants are in a different situation which table 5-18 clearly shows. While 48 per cent of the new enterprises state they face problems, seven out of ten old bread plants state they face problems. Demand, i.e. limited purchasing power, and competition pose obstacles to their marketing activities. The diversified structure of marketing channels for old bread plants with a relatively high share of middlemen can be regarded as a reaction to this situation.

Table 5-18: Problems of the Bread Producing Units with Selling at Specific Locations in the Irkutsk Oblast

	Market oriented cluster		Non-market oriented cluster		Additional system		Old plants	
	Number	%	Number	%	Number	%	Number	%
Yes	51	44.7	3	4.5	10		7	70
No	64	55.6	64	95.5	20		3	30
Missing	1		0		2			
Problems								
Competition	25	54.3	1		2	20	3	
Transportation costs	2	4.3	1					
Demand	18	39.1			7	70	3	
Others	6	13			1	10		

Source: Survey 2000

5.3.4 General Criteria

So far the description has discussed criteria of the enterprise groups which are related to their position in markets and on the possible impact of transition features. Now the discussion will turn to characteristics that are of a more general nature. However, their shape can be expected to be different between the groups, too.

Size While the size measured in number of workers will clearly show some differences between old bread plants and new enterprises and the additional system, the difference between these two and between the two clusters is not that obvious. However, assuming that there is a positive relation between age of a production unit and size and, given their former function, the enterprises of the additional system can be expected to be larger than the new enterprises. Unfortunately, due to a very high number of missing values in the data on production volumes, it is not possible to calculate the market share of each of the groups, which would have been particularly interesting in the context of the competition between new market oriented enterprises and old bread plants. The same refers to figures on turnover. Hence, the description has to be solely based on the number of workers.

Figure 5-2: Share of Workers Employed in Enterprises of the Different Groups

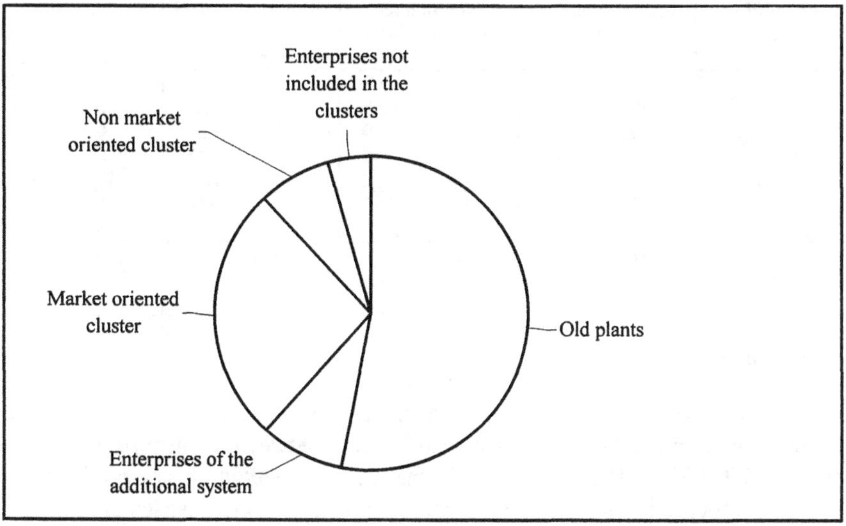

Source: Survey 2000; author's own drawing

However, figure 5-2 shows the share of workers of each group of enterprises in the total number of enterprises. Due to a high share of missing values for old plants, the average workforce for the missing seven entities was taken as the actual number of their workforce. Regarding this indicator, new bakeries have a share of 38 per cent in the total workforce which is fairly high as it can be expected that old plants are overstaffed. Hence, the market share of new enterprises is expected to be high, too.

The number of workers in the market oriented cluster of the new bakeries is on average significantly higher than the number of workers of the enterprises of the non-market oriented cluster. However, the number of enterprises that employ more than 20 workers is surprisingly high, and hence raises the average. The class of enterprises with 16-20 workers is not occupied in the non-market oriented cluster while the class for the market oriented cluster contains ten enterprises. Hence, even ignoring the maximum numbers of workers in the market oriented cluster, a higher number of workers in the market oriented cluster remains.

Table 5-19: Size of Bread Producing Enterprises in the Irkutsk Oblast in 2000

Number of workers	Market oriented cluster		Non-market oriented cluster		Additional system		Old plants	
	Number	%	Number	%	Number	%	Number	%
1-5	43	38	37	55.2	12	37.5	0	0
6-10	39	34.5	24	35.8	12	37.5	0	0
11-15	10	8.8	6	9	3	9.37	0	0
16-20	10	8.8	0	0	1	3.12	0	0
More than 20	11	9.7	0	0	4	12.5	10	100
Total	113	100	67	100	32	100	10	
Missing	3				0	0	0	
Minimum	1		2		2		43	
Maximum	170		15		170		791	
Mean	12.2		5.8		14.28		225.4	

Source: Survey 2000

Assortment: Also the comparison of the assortments, the number of sorts and changes in assortments reveal strong differences between the groups as shown in tables 5-20 – 5-22. The enterprises in the market oriented cluster produce more products groups, i.e. in addition to bread rolls, cakes and pastries etc., than the enterprises of the non-market oriented cluster. While 55.2 per cent of the market oriented cluster produce a second sort with rolls as the most popular and even 19.0 per cent produce cakes and pastries which requires specific technologies, only 11.9 per cent of the bakeries in the non-market oriented cluster produce a second group. Furthermore, the average number of sorts produced by the enterprises in the market oriented cluster is much higher with 6.92 per cent than in the non-market oriented cluster with 1.71 per cent. For both criteria the enterprises of the additional system are comparable to the market oriented cluster while the figures for the old bread plants are, as expected, much higher.

The change in the assortments underlines the market orientation and non-market orientation of the groups. While almost all old bread plants have added sorts and 38.1 per cent of the bakeries of the market oriented cluster have added sorts and only 9.5 per cent have removed sorts, there was little dynamic in the assortment of the enterprises of the non-market oriented cluster. Only 26.8 per cent state a change in the assortment since they started their business. The position of the additional system again is not clear. Around 40 per cent have removed sorts from their assortment while 28 have added sorts and 25 have not changed the assortment at all.

Table 5-20: Assortments of the Bread Producing Enterprises in the Irkutsk Oblast in 2000

	Market oriented cluster		Non-market oriented cluster		Additional system		Old plants	
	Number	% of cases	Number	% of cases	Number	% of cases	Number	% of cases
Bread	116	100.0	67	100.0	32	100.0	10	100
Rolls	64	55.2	8	11.9	17	53.1	10	100
Baton	23	19.8	5	7.5	9	28.1	3	30
Cakes and pastries	22	19.0	4	6.0	4	12.5	9	90
Pasta	3	2.6	1	1.5	1	3.1	6	60

Source: Survey 2000

Table 5-21: Number of Sorts of the Bread Producing Enterprises in the Irkutsk Oblast in 2000

Number of sorts	Market oriented cluster		Non-market oriented cluster		Additional system		Old plants	
	Number	%	Number	%	Number	%	Number	%
1-5	65	62.5	62	98.4	23	71.87	0	0
6-10	20	19.23	1	1.6	7	21.87	0	0
11-15	6	5.76	0	0	1	3.12	0	0
16-20	3	2.88	0	0	1	3.12	0	0
More than 20	10	9.56	0	0	0	0	10	100
Total	104	89.7	63	94	32	100	10	
Missing	12	10.3	4	6	0	0	0	
Minimum	1		1		1		5	
Maximum	57		6		16		94	
Mean	6.92		1.71		4.46		39.9	

Source: Survey 2000

Table 5-22: Changes in the Assortments of Bread Producing Units in the Irkutsk Oblast since Start of the Business or since 1992.

	Market oriented cluster		Non-market oriented cluster		Additional system		Old plants	
	Number	%	Number	%	Number	%	Number	%
No change	57	49.1	48	71.6	8	25	3	30
Added sorts	45	38.1	7	10.4	9	28.1	6	60
Removed sorts	11	9.5	9	13.4	13	40.6	1	10
Added and removed sorts	2	1.7	2	3.0	2	6.3	0	0
Total	115		66		32		10	
Missing	1		1		0		0	

Source: Survey 2000

Financial figures: The only reliable data with regard to the financial figures of enterprise activities is the cost structure. Data on turnover, expenses or profits show high numbers of missing values, and the reliability of the remainder can be questioned. The only statement that can be made from anecdotal evidence is that bakeries that operate in markets are profitable and some are even highly profitable. This gives reason to the enterprises to keep financial figures secret or manipulate them. On the other hand, it has to be stated that some enterprises do not know the basic figures of their activity. In some cases it has taken the bookkeepers hours to calculate the figures. They were not available in internal documents. This was not due to the financial year as figures can be expected to be available on a monthly basis which would have been easy to calculate.

The cost structures of the three groups differ only slightly. However, while the structures for the non-market oriented cluster, the additional system and old bread plants are almost identical in important indicators like raw materials and wages, they are different for the enterprises of the market oriented cluster. The average share of raw materials for enterprises of the market oriented cluster are higher, while the average share of wages are lower.

Table 5-23: Cost Structures of the Bread Producing Units in the Irkutsk Oblast

	Market oriented cluster			Non-market oriented cluster			Additional system			Old plants		
	N	Mean	Std. Dev	N	Mean	Std. Dev	N	Mean	Std. Dev	N	Mean	Std. Dev
Share of raw materials	95	64.08	10.39	59	60.92	15.42	29	60.15	12.76	9	59.56	9.54
Share of other materials	94	3.29	4.52	59	3.36	13.22	28	2.83	5.68	8	4.01	7.14
Share of electricity, water and gas	94	3.86	3.65	59	3.68	5.17	28	7.21	6.51	9	7.67	7.11
Share of depreciation	94	1.77	2.41	59	3.27	3.67	29	2.95	5.19	9	1.70	2.15
Share of rent	93	2.87	5.04	59	6.071 E-02	.40	28	6.071 E-02	.30	7	.00	.00
Share of transport	94	7.03	6.51	59	6.53	7.33	29	5.76	7.01	9	5.87	2.69
Share of distribution	93	1.15	2.79	59	.11	.78	28	6.071 E-02	.22	9	1.56	2.35
Share of wages	95	12.19	6.46	59	14.74	9.85	29	14.71	9.17	9	16.91	6.86
Share of others	94	3.90	6.57	59	5.75	6.11	28	6.72	8.34	9	3.07	4.77

Source: Survey 2000

5.4 Summary

The comparison of the descriptive statistics of almost all variables revealed significant differences between the four groups of enterprises that were compared. Particularly, the differences between the two groups of new enterprises are considerable. All indicators reveal the market orientation and non-market orientation of the groups respectively. When comes to the old production units, the bread plants can, according to the criteria described, be assigned to market oriented enterprises, while the facilities of the additional system are ambiguous in their nature. However, in contrast to the large plants they do not show many adjustments to market conditions.

Particularly important for the aspect of market development is the role that small enterprises play on the adjustment of the large plants. The large plants report that they face strong competition from small enterprises in addition to strong constraints from the purchasing power of the population, and react by making changes in production. However, this holds true only for some of the large plants. An explanation for this will be given in the next chapter. Nonetheless, taking the share of market oriented bakeries in the total workforce as proxy for market share, and assuming that the old plants are overstaffed, the new market oriented bakeries already play an important role in the market.

Though their share of the total market, given the share in the total workforce, is much less, the description of the new bakeries that are characterized as non-market oriented leads to an important conclusion. It very much supports the result of chapter four that there is a sharp urban-rural divide in market development. The bakeries of this cluster are almost entirely located in rural areas, they are smaller, produce only a minimum number of sorts and show no signs of reactions to markets.

6. The Resulting Pattern: The Organization of Spatial Markets in a Segmented Industry in Transition

6.1 Introduction

Over a long period of time studies in industrial organization were dominated by the structure-conduct-performance approach that goes back to the influential work of Bain (1954). The basic idea in this literature is that structure (the level of concentration) determines conduct (the degree of collusion) and conduct determines performance (profitability). Structure in turn is shaped by the influence of barriers to entry like scale economies, levels of advertising or R&D[75]. Authors agree that the huge bulk of studies that emerged as the consequence of this approach has produced very useful stylized facts. However, despite severe endogeneity problems in measurement, the approach has failed to establish a relationship between the factors that goes beyond correlation. Furthermore, the insights brought by the game-theoretic literature on the same subject indicate that the great variety of factors that are crucial for the explanation of market structure question the meaning of cross-industry analysis in industrial organization[76].

John Sutton (1991) brought a new strand into the thinking on industrial organization with the concept of endogenous and exogenous sunk costs to explain the market structure of industries. The starting point of his theory is the observation of statistically relevant similarities across industries, especially in the relation between market size and market structure. In his view it would be going too far to abandon the above- mentioned strand of research in industrial organization. However, the observed regularities need some more profound theoretical backing. The basic observation for the development of the theory is that market structure is similar across different countries for the same industry while a regularity in market structure across industries cannot be observed.

Sutton distinguishes between exogenous and endogenous sunk costs. All entrants into a market have to incur exogenous sunk costs which basically represent set-up costs of a plant of minimum efficient scale. These costs are exogenous to the firm's decision as they are basically determined by technology. Endogenous sunk costs are costs like advertising and R&D which are choice variables to the firms. In industries where sunk costs are exogenous and firms offer a homoge-

75 Sutton, 1991, p. 4.
76 Schmalensee, 1989, p.951 ff; Tirole, 1998, p. 2 ff.

nous product, the theory predicts a negative relation of concentration and the ratio of market size to set-up costs and a positive relation of concentration to the toughness of competition in the industry. The equilibrium concentration in the market is shaped by these two factors. In the case of differentiated products with exogenous sunk costs, as is the case for example in spatial differentiation, the theory predicts an indefinitely low level of concentration with an increase in market size relative to set-up costs. In contrast to this, endogenous sunk costs put a lower bound to concentration because endogenous sunk costs like advertising have an effect on demand. A larger market size induces an escalation of advertising outlays by competing firms which in turn leads to higher sunk costs. Hence in some industries the scope for fragmentation is limited.

In the context of transition Brown & Brown (1998) present a study in the tradition of the structure-conduct-performance approach. They argue to overcome the basic measurement problems of endogeneity between profitability and market structure because the Russian market structure was determined by planners and as a result is exogenous to profitability. However, this approach ignores the development of market structure and the role of small businesses in this development. The present study focuses more on the emerging market structure than on profitability considerations and subsequently follows the sunk cost argumentation. The bakery sector can easily be identified as an exogenous sunk cost industry and with this characterization it clearly remains in the traditional view of market structure analysis as coined by Bain (1954)[77]. There the simple formula for market structure can be represented as

$N = S / m$, where N is the number of efficient-size firms that fit into the industry, S the market size and m the minimum efficient scale

which is nothing else than the prediction of a negative relation between concentration and the ratio of market size to set-up costs given that the minimum efficient scale is constant and set-up costs are proportional to enterprise size. However, the idea of exogenous sunk costs will be kept in the present analysis as Sutton adds one more important aspect to the discussion, that is price competition in the market. As explained in chapter three, according to the constant returns to scale assumption in the bakery sector, the development of a large number of new bakeries is expected and has occurred as shown in the preceding two chapters. The emergence of new bakeries is not only relevant in terms of reallocation and increased efficiency in production; they are also crucial for the development of competition and entrepreneurship. However, this can only be realized if the new

77 Kwoka & White, 2001, p. 26.

bakeries have entry to large markets where old plants are already operating and if the new bakeries themselves behave in a competitive manner. As seen in chapter five, this is only partly the case. The objective of this chapter is to analyze the development of market structure and the influence of the acting old enterprises and the role of non-market oriented bakeries on the predicted market-size-market-structure relation.

The analysis of the Swedish driving school industry by Asplund (1998) and Asplund & Sandin (1997) serves as a reference study for the market structure development of a spatially fragmented exogenous sunk cost industry in a market economy. The similarities of the industries in terms of characteristics that determine market structure allow a comparison of the two. The product in the driving school industry is a driving lesson which is a non-transportable good similar to bread. A driving lesson can be regarded as transportable only in the sense that students travel distances to receive the lesson. This is going to occur in situations where persons work in a place other than where they live and consume the driving lesson in the settlement of their working place. This can occur in bread production, too. Hence, the driving school industry is a spatially fragmented industry like the bread baking industry. In both industries it requires some sunk set-up costs to open a business and some minimum fixed costs, for instance office space and a car or production space and an oven, mixing machine etc. These fixed costs can be recouped when scaling down or with exit. Product differentiation is minor in the driving school industry. It could be large in the bread sector, but the degree of product differentiation is still negligible in the bread baking sector in the Irkutsk Oblast. The two basic principles of viability and stability[78] count for the industry configuration which warrant that a firm's profits do cover set-up costs and fixed costs and that no business opportunity will be left open[79].

The hypothesis on market structure in the spatially segmented exogenous sunk cost industry is a negative relationship between market size and concentration. Furthermore, the hypotheses applies that firm sizes within a market are equal and that firms in large markets tend to be larger. This argument at the same time explains that a skewed firm size distribution can be explained by a skewed size distribution of the underlying market structure. Asplund (1998) shows these regularities for the driving school industry in Sweden. Hence, it should be possible to establish the same relations in the bread baking sector in the Irkutsk Oblast if the old production pattern and transition phenomena do not interfere with the relation.

---

78 compare to chapter three.
79 Sutton, 1997.

According to the hypotheses on market structure development in chapter three, the hypotheses on the relation between market structure, firm size and market size have to be adjusted. In large markets where old plants are operating concentration will decrease during transition. However, concentration will still be high as large enterprises will keep the largest market shares. Where old bread plants have the possibility to prevent entry, for example through direct closeness with the administration, concentration will remain high and competition will be hampered. It follows that the negative relation of market size to concentration remains because small monopolies develop while concentration ratios in large markets will decrease. However, compared to a market economy result, without dominating old bread plants the relation is weakened.

Furthermore, the existence of non-market oriented bakeries can distort the positive relation of market size to firm size. The production purpose of these enterprises is the provision of the population with bread and not profits. As a result the mechanisms that lead to equilibria in firm sizes, i.e. the interplay of market size and price competition, do not function for these enterprises. Notwithstanding, in markets of a size that suffices for a monopoly the same size structure could be expected as capacity building should be in compliance with demand. On the other hand, as bread is a part of the paid wages, demand will react on prices to a lesser extent. Additionally, the search for a location though within the municipalities the agricultural enterprise covers could be of a more accidental nature.

6.2 Market Structure, Market Size Distribution and Firm Size Distribution

The analysis of the relation between market structure, firm size distribution and market size distribution on the one hand and the interference of the old production pattern and transition phenomena into this relationship on the other hand requires several steps. Firstly, the settlement structure as a representative of market size distribution will be described. Secondly, the relation between market size and concentration will be tested using some descriptive statistics and concentration measures. In a third step, the markets will be analyzed separately to show spatial clustering of the different enterprise types and the coexistence or non-coexistence of new and old enterprises. The next step will bring the different factors together in a regression analysis on market structure. The last subsection will take a look at the price levels within and between markets.

6.2.1 The Number and Size of Markets

The settlement structure of the particular region reflects the number and size of markets. As already mentioned, most parts of the Irkutsk Oblast are sparsely populated while around 80 per cent of the population is concentrated in cities and towns. This poses certain limitations on the analysis. The settlement statistics available for the year 1996 report settlements of only one person. As it is likely that some of these settlements do not exist any more and bakeries are not going to appear in settlements of only one person, this level is not meaningful to the analysis. The statistics aggregate the population of a number of neighboring settlements to a rural municipality. These municipalities are regarded as markets in the following analysis. Hence, a rural municipality represents a market though the distances between the settlements within the municipality can be significant. It has to be mentioned that migration into rural areas occurred during transition as well as the dying of small settlements in remote areas. Consequently, the statistics of 1996 do not perfectly reflect the picture in 2000.

The Irkutsk Oblast is divided into 33 raions out of which 24 were covered by the survey. Within the raions lie 450 municipalities and 1570 settlements. The number of municipalities include urban as well as rural municipalities. Out of these, the survey covered 353 municipalities and 1342 settlements respectively.

Table 6-1: Coverage of Settlements and Raions Covered by the Survey 2000

	Raions (Districts)	Municipalities	Settlements
Total	33	450	1570
Covered by the survey	24, 9 cities separately counted	353	1342
Bakeries observed in	24, 9 cities separately counted	139	145
In per cent of the surveyed	100%	38.5%	10.8%
Minimum population		171	1
Maximum population		584900	584900
Minimum population where bakery observed		488	44

Source: Committee for State Statistics of the Irkutsk Oblast, 1997

As given in table 6-1 a bakery is observed in only 38.5 per cent of the surveyed municipalities. The smallest entity, where a bakery is observed has a population of 488, while the largest is the city of Irkutsk with 584,900 inhabitants. Cities of this size are actually comprised of a number of sub-markets, which are loosely connected by the traveling of consumers. Nevertheless, in the context here, cities will be regarded as one unit because in the view of old plants cities count as a single market.

It follows that in 214 of the surveyed municipalities, there is no bakery at present. The size distribution of these markets is interesting. If the size of most of these municipalities lies below the size of the smallest municipality with a bakery, the minimum scale for viability of a bakery could easily explain the high share. However, it turns out that only 8.4 per cent of the markets without a bakery have less population than the smallest market with a bakery. The market size at which in each larger settlement a bakery is located amounts to 9800 while there is no regularity in the presence or absence of bakeries for settlements of smaller size.

However, allowing for the marketing locations of the enterprises, the picture of provision with bread in the region changes. Out of the new firms and the sample of small old firm 43.44 per cent answer that they sell to a second location, 18.44 per cent to a third location, 9.8 per cent to a fourth location, six per cent to a fifth location and one per cent to a sixth location. However, the picture is not very precise as the firms also indicated deliveries to 'other villages', 'to the whole raion' or to the respective enterprises. Part of the low regional coverage can be explained by this fact.

The number of enterprises, which indicate they deliver to other villages or the whole raion amounts to 23, the number of enterprises that deliver all villages the agricultural enterprise covers amounts to 11. The number of settlements that have bread delivered is roughly 100. Among the additional villages, only one appears to which two enterprises deliver. Some enterprises deliver to locations where other bakeries produce and thereby increase competition, but looking at municipalities these deliveries are negligible. Moreover, the average share of production volume that is sold at the location of production is 84.45 per cent for the new enterprises and 75.86 per cent for the old additional system. Consequently, the general picture of market structure and competition will not change, allowing for all sellers in the market. The exceptions are three markets where five or six additional sellers appear which increases the number of sellers to a degree that is in compliance with the market sizes and, furthermore, indicates a strong competitive relation between two of these locations as they lie close to each other and all producers in one or other location sell in both markets. For these reasons, the following analysis of bread markets in the Irkutsk Oblast is based on the producers in the markets and not on the sellers in the markets.

For this the first step is to check the skewness of size distribution of markets and of firm size distribution because the above-explained assumption of a skewed firm size distribution is based on the existence of a skewed market size distribution. As can easily be recognized from figure 6-1, the market size distribution is skewed and, furthermore, the statistics in table 6-2 approve also a skewed firm size distribution.

Figure 6-1: Market Size Distribution in the Irkutsk Oblast

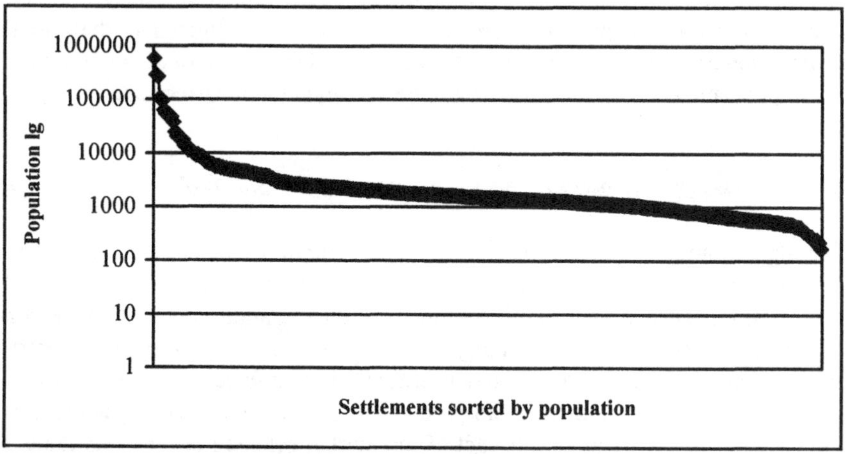

Source: Committee for State Statistics of the Irkutsk Oblast, 1997.

Table 6-2: Skewness of Firm Size Distribution and Market Size Distribution

				Skewness	
	N	Mean	Std. Deviation	Statistic	Std. Error
Population	136	15074.13	60851.57	7.389	.208
Workers per firms	253	19.96	63.16	8.780	.153

Source: Survey 2000, Committee for State Statistics of the Irkutsk Oblast, 1997.

The skewness is much starker than in the example of the Swedish driving school industry. This is due to two facts. In the Swedish example, the largest municipalities were excluded because of the above-mentioned reason of segmented markets within these municipalities. Furthermore, the strong skewness of the enterprise size distribution in the Irkutsk bread sector results from the large size of the old bread plants. Therefore, it remains to show the relation of a market size - firm size relation for the new enterprises. The correlation of market size and firm size shows a significant positive correlation for the enterprises of the market oriented cluster (0.358, N=116) and a non-significant positive correlation for the non-market oriented cluster (0.112, N=67). Though the different results can be due to the small sample sizes, they suggest the following interpretation. While market oriented bakeries tend to be larger in larger markets the size of non-market oriented bakeries is independent of the market size. Hence, the above assumed market based mechanisms do not work for these bakeries.

The different role of bakeries of the market oriented and non-market oriented cluster for the development of markets should also be reflected in their spatial distribution and clustering in single markets. The distribution of different types of bread producing units over markets will be shown in the next section.

6.2.2 Market Structure, Previous Production Pattern and Transition Influences

Among the municipalities where only one production unit can be found which adds up to a total of 94, 16 are represented by enterprises of cluster one, 40 by enterprises of cluster two, 19 by enterprises of the old additional system and 4 are old bread plants, which are regularly located in towns. This can be interpreted as follows: around 60 per cent of the new enterprises that were characterized as non-market oriented are the only bread production unit in their location, while this is the case for only around 14 per cent of the market oriented bakeries. Adding the enterprises in locations where two entities of the same cluster are present, 75 per cent of the units of cluster two are present in administrations where there is no other type of bread baking facility while this is the case for only 27.4 per cent of the market oriented bakeries. This supports the correlation results of the preceding section which indicate that part of the capacity building is not demand driven, and hence indicate a distorted allocation of production.

Furthermore, it provides evidence that, as expected, areas developed that are isolated from market development. However, 25 per cent of enterprises remain which were characterized as non-market oriented that are located in markets with bakeries of a different type. Where the combination is with enterprises of the old additional system this is still in compliance with the prediction of areas that are completely cut off from market development. This is the case for another 7.4 per cent of the enterprises of cluster two. The remainder of the group is located in the same markets as market oriented bakeries. These markets are either large towns in grain producing areas or larger settlements in rural areas which are closer to market development due to their function as a district center or their close proximity to towns.

Four administrations where only one old bread plant is located give rise to the hypothesis that old bread plants hamper the entry of new firms into the market. Though it is very unlikely that no other bakery emerged, even a small number of new bakeries in these markets would support the prediction. Even more so is adding the enterprise structures of the markets where the remaining old bread plants are located. One is located in a market of the combination of (4, 2, 1)[80], two in the combination of (4, 1, 1, 1) and (4, 1, 1, .) respectively and another two in the combinations of (4, 4, 3, 1, 1, .) and of (4, 2, 1, 1, 1 .) respectively. The remaining five old bread plants are located in markets with 14 or more production units out of which three can be characterized as markets where old bread plants dominate but are competing with new bakeries. In the remaining market, the enterprise structure is not that clear as a relatively large number of enterprises of cluster two are present (4, 3, 2, 2, 2, 2, 9x1, .).

Among the administrations where old enterprises are located and no or just a few new enterprises have developed are the largest cities of the region, which form the center of the region (compare figure 2-1). Hence, these markets will distort the market-size market-structure relation. Among the markets where no competition has developed around the old bread plants are also cities that lie next to Lake Baikal whose only connection with the region is to Irkutsk given the physical environment (landscape). However, in all other towns competition around the old bread plants has developed. These towns lie distant from the center where plant management might already be less powerful to prevent entry by competitors through existing links with the administration. One market has developed where five bakeries are located that are characterized as market oriented (1, 1, 1, 1, 1).

6.2.3 Market Size and Concentration

The results of the preceding section give very strong evidence that the market-size market-structure relation is strongly distorted and, moreover, that firm size distribution within markets is not equal. The first step is to see which market structures exist. Judging purely by the number of firms in the market, the distribution as given in table 6-3 can be observed[81]. It could be expected from the market size distribution that in most of the markets only one bakery operates, and hence around 70 per cent of the observed markets are monopolies. Duopolies

---

80 The numbers in brackets describe the market structure and have to be read as follows: each number stands for one enterprise in the market. Four describes old bread plants, three represents enterprises of the old additional system, two for bakeries that belong to cluster two as identified in chapter four, and one for bakeries that belong to cluster one as identified in chapter four. A dot represents an enterprise with unknown cluster. 9x1 means nine enterprises of cluster one.

81 It is not possible to base the analysis on data on production volumes which would have been interesting in the context of location. Unfortunately, the data on production volumes contains too many missing values to conduct a reliable analysis.

make up about 20 per cent of all markets while in the remainder of the markets more than two and up to 17 bakeries operate.

Table 6-3: Market Structure of Bread Markets in the Irkutsk Oblast

Market structure	No. of markets	
	Number	%
Monopoly	94	67.6
Duopoly	27	19.4
Oligopoly	14	10.0
Competitive	4	2.8
Total	139	99.8

Source: Survey 2000; author's own calculations

As shown in the preceding section, structures like a dominant firm with a fringe have developed and a reduced entry of new entities has occurred in markets where subsequently competition to old plants remains limited. This should have a strong influence on concentration in the markets. The traditional measure for market concentration is the Herfindahl Index which is calculated for the present purpose as given in the following equation:

$$HERFINDAHL_i = \sum_{k=1}^{FIRMSi} (FWORKERS_{i,k} / MWORKERS_i)^2 ,$$

where *FWORKERS* is the number of workers for each firm in the market and *MWORKERS* the total number of workers in the market. For some of the large enterprises the number of workers was missing. But since these figures are crucial for the analysis of concentration, the number of workers was added according to the average number of workers of enterprises in the center which are larger, and of enterprises more distant from the center which are smaller, for four old enterprises in total.

The Herfindahl indices (henceforth HI) for markets with two bakeries range from 0.5 which indicates equal firm sizes to 0.992 which means a very large unit and a very small unit in the same market. The mean is 0.625. Hence, the prediction of an equal firm size distribution is not found. The results for markets where three or more firms operate are given in table 6-4.

Table 6-4: Herfindahl Indices for Oligopolies and Competitive Markets in the Irkutsk Oblast

Number of firms in the market (firms)	HI	HI – 1/firms	Number of firms in the market (firms)	HI	HI – 1/firms
4	0.252	0.002	17	0.167	0.108
5	0.211	0.011	14	0.186	0.114
3	0.350	0.016	3	0.449	0.116
4	0.285	0.035	16	0.189	0.127
6	0.202	0.036	6	0.348	0.182
3	0.369	0.036	4	0.649	0.399
4	0.344	0.094	6	0.594	0.427
14	0.178	0.106			

Source: Survey 2000; author's own calculations

The concentration measured as the deviation of the Herfindahl index from the minimum size of enterprises given equal distribution (HI – 1/firms) differs significantly for the more fragmented markets from almost perfect fragmentation (0.002) for a market with four firms to strong concentration (0.427) for a market with six firms operating.

According to the above-explained theoretical considerations, the concentration is negatively correlated to market size. For the present example this relation holds taking all markets in the industry. The correlation coefficient of HI to population is –0.312. However, monopolies are strongly represented in the industry. Running the correlation for markets where two or more firms are operating the relation breaks down. Though it remains negative it is no longer significant. Much of the concentration, and hence the non-equal distribution of firm sizes within markets, can be explained by the co-existence of old and new firms.

It remains to analyse the firm sizes within markets only for new enterprises. The concentration for all markets where old and new enterprises are present has been calculated on the base of only new firms. The resulting HI subtracting the minimum size again reveals a diverse pattern: the lowest concentration is 0.007 which indicates almost perfect fragmentation; the highest is 0.15 and indicates an unequal firm size distribution. Hence, the market-size–firm size rule is not only distorted by the presence of old enterprises but also by the emergence of new firms in itself.

6.2.4 Determinants of Market Structure of a Spatially Segmented Exogenous Sunk Cost Industry in Transition

As found in table 6-1, out of 353 markets, there are no bakeries in 217 markets. Therefore, it is unlikely to be a random sample as these markets may be very small, close to other markets, or have high costs. For this, in the empirical estimation, the present chapter employs Heckman's (1979) two-stage procedure to correct for the possible sample selection bias. In the first stage is the presence of a bakery in a market that equals one if a market has a bakery, and is zero otherwise. In the second stage, it is the total number of bakeries that belong to a market, given that there exists a bakery.

The presence of a bakery - the discrete state: To test for the presence of a bakery in a market, here, the approach is to augment a standard cross-sectional function to include a dummy indicating whether a market had an old firm or not. The logic behind the inclusion of the presence of an old enterprise is to examine the impact of the old system on the transition process. Let E_i represent a dummy variable that equals 1 if the *i*th market is characterized by the presence of an old enterprise, and zero otherwise. It follows that the presence of a bakery in *i*th market depend on E_i, and a vector of observed characteristics X_i, and can be described by the latent variable model:

$$F_i^* = \alpha' E_i + \beta' X_i + \varepsilon_i,$$

where F_i^* is the expected state of the presence of a bakery, ε_i is a normally distributed error term with mean zero and unit variance, and α and β are parameters to be estimated. Assuming for each market *i* a dummy variable F_i that expresses the bivariate state of a market's bakery presence status, the conditional probability that for market *i* given E_i and X_i, one observes $F_i = 1$, (presence of a bakery in a market) is given by

$$(2) \quad P(F_i = 1 | E_i, X_i) = P(\alpha' E_i + \beta' X_i + \varepsilon_{1i} \geq 0) = F(\frac{\alpha' E_i + \beta' X_i}{\sigma_1}).$$

The total number of bakeries: The total number of bakeries observed in a market can be expressed as a function of market characteristics denoted by Y_i and can be described by:

(3) $TF_i = \gamma' Y_i + \varepsilon_{2i}$

Here TF_i is the total number of bakeries observed in a market, Y_i is the vector of market characteristics, ε_{3i} is a normally distributed error term with mean zero and unit variance, and γ is the vector of parameters to be estimated.

Since the total number of bakeries TF_i in a particular market i is preceded by presence of a bakery F_i^*, one observes TF_i only for markets for which $F_i^* \geq 0$. Following Heckman (1979), the study corrects for this sample selection bias. Taking into consideration the issue of sample selection bias, (3) can be rewritten for the sub-sample of markets for which $F_i^* \geq 0$:

(4) $E(TF_i | Y_i, F_i^* \geq 0) = \gamma' Y_i + E(\varepsilon_{2i} | Y_i, F_i^* \geq 0)$

Denoting ρ as the correlation coefficient between ε_{1i} and ε_{2i}:

(5) $E(\varepsilon_{3i} | Y_i, F_i^* \geq o) = \rho\lambda_i$

where $\lambda_i = c(A_i)/C(-A_i)$, $A_i = -[\beta' X_i]$, and c and C are the standard normal pdf and cdf respectively. Introducing the correction term, equation (4) can be rewritten as:[82]

(6) $TF_i = \gamma' Y_i + \rho\lambda_i + \tilde{\varepsilon}_{2i}$

where $E(\tilde{\varepsilon}_{2i} | F_i^* \geq 0) = 0$ and $E(\tilde{\varepsilon}_{2i}^2 | F_i^* \geq 0) = \tau_i^2$, and $\tau_i^2 = 1 + \rho^2 \lambda_i (A - \lambda_i)$. Dividing equation (6) by $\tau_i (\tau_i > 0)$, the estimating equation for the sub-sample of markets with $F_i^* \geq 0$ is:

(7) $TF_i = \gamma'(Y_i / \tau_i) + \rho(\lambda_i / \tau_i) + \varepsilon_{3i}$

where $E(\varepsilon_{3i} | F_i^* \geq 0) = 0$ and $E(\varepsilon_{3i}^2 | F_i^* \geq 0) = 1$.

82 For a complete derivation see Heckman, 1979, pp. 156-77.

Table 6-5: Two-stage-least-square Estimation on Market Structure; Summary statistics

Variables	Min	Max	Mean	Std. Dev.
Dependent variables:				
Presence of firm (1 = present)	0	1	0.38	0.49
Number of firms per market	0	17	0.73	1.83
Explanatory variables:				
Presence of old enterprise (1 = present)	0	1	0.12	0.32
Population	171	584900	6923	38559
Average household income 1995 in roubles	300	1257.5	488.2	167.2
Area under grain 1995	0	59260	31755.8	16800
Volume of wage arrears 1997	3	597.2	197	44.1
Distance to next location with bakery in km	0	175	26.75	28.97
Dummy for non-monopolies (0 = monopoly)	0	1	0.12	0.33

Source: Committee for State Statistics of the Irkutsk Oblast 1997, 1999; Survey 2000, author's own calculations.

Table 6-6: Two-stage-least-square Estimation on Market Structure; Estimation Results

Variables	Coefficient	Std. Err.
Population	-4.65e-07	3.86e-06
Average household income 1995	.0002945	.0006389
Presence of old firm	1.826971*	.2638067
Area under grain 1995	-5.55e-06	5.90e-06
Volume of wage arrears 1997	.0162705*	.0034321
Constant	.3254867	.4274814
Select		
Distance to next location with bakery	-.0293885*	.0081784
Dummy for non-monopolies	1.946446*	.
Presence of old firms	5.069288*	.
Constant	4.819627	.

* significant at the 5%-level.

Source: Committee for State Statistics of the Irkutsk Oblast 1997, 1999; Survey 2000, own calculations.

Table 6-6 reports the Heckman selection model. The presence of an old firm as well as the distance from the next bakery have influence on the presence of a new bakery in the market which was estimated in the first stage. The distance from the next bakery shows a negative sign. Hence, the further the next bakery the more likely a new bakery is to emerge. Regarding distance, it should be noted that the results of chapter four are repeated. Furthermore, it should be noted that the average distance to the market with the next bakery is approximately 27 km which is less than the possible distance assumed by planners (compare chapter 3.2.3).

Regarding the estimation of the number of firms in the market the results are as could be expected from the descriptions above. Neither population nor average income show an influence on the number of firms in the market. Population even reveals a negative coefficient which would indicate that the larger the market the smaller is the expected number of firms in the market. It follows that the market-size – market-structure rule is not found according to the regression results which is in compliance with the observations in the subsections above.

Coming to the transition factors influencing the market structure, area under grain as a proxy for grain producing enterprises does not show any effect on the number of firms in the market, while the wage arrears do. They show a positive sign which indicates that the higher the transition influence the higher the probable number of firms in the market. As wage arrears stand as a proxy for distorted demand, the positive coefficient supports the result of a complete distortion of the market-structure–market-size rule.

6.3 Market Structure and Prices

The criterion where market structure should be well reflected is price. Unfortunately, the prices for a homogenous product, i.e. same recipe and same weight, were available from only 96 enterprises, which sell at 87 locations. Though this considerably limits the possibilities of analysis, some insights into the price schemes are possible.

6.3.1 Price Relations in the Bread Sector in the Irkutsk Oblast

According to economic theory in competitive markets, prices are expected to be lower than in oligopolies or monopolies. However, the discussion in chapter three resulted in hypotheses of a distorted price scheme due to the transition phenomena. In this scenario prices in competitive markets are expected to be higher than prices in markets where non-market oriented bakeries operate. Furthermore, prices of market oriented enterprises in a monopoly position are expected to be higher than prices of market oriented enterprises in competitive markets. The analysis of markets in the preceding sections has shown that most of the market oriented new bakeries are located in duopolies, oligopolies or competitive markets, while most of the enterprises of the non-market oriented cluster take a monopoly position which is in compliance with their subsistence character. Hence, a comparison of the prices of the two groups should already provide some evidence on these hypotheses. The results of the comparison are given in table 6-7[83].

Table 6-7: Comparison of Prices of Bakeries of Cluster One and Cluster Two

Cluster	Minimum	Maximum	Mean	Std Dev/Error
Market oriented cluster	3.43	6.69	4.63	0.7547
Non- market oriented cluster	2.77	5.08	3.82	0.6366
Independent sample t-test				
T	4.84	Mean difference	.8023	
F	62.154	Standard error	.1655	
Sig (2-tailed)	.000			

Source: Survey 2000, author's own calculations

The prices of the enterprises of the two groups differ significantly. As expected, the prices of the non-market oriented cluster are lower than the prices of the market-oriented cluster. This is the case for the minimum price observed, the maximum price observed in each group, and the mean.

The price span given in the table at the same time represents the span of prices in the whole region. The highest observed price is 2.4 times higher than the lowest price. Given the high number of local markets and the enormous distances between these markets, along with the diversity of enterprises and their production goals, this difference is not surprising.

A comparison of the average prices of markets with three or more producers should give an idea of the functioning of the competitive markets in the region.

Table 6-8 reveals that even in local markets the price differences are rather high. The most plausible explanation would be that each of the markets in the table represents several segmented markets. However, the size of some of the markets as well as Russian reality argues against it. Given the high constraints in purchasing power it can be expected that households search for cheaper prices even for bread, and a higher integration of markets at least in the smaller cities like Osa or Sima can be expected.

83 All prices are in Roubles. The sort of bread for which prices are compared is bread second sort, 0.65kg.

Table 6-8: Observed Bread Prices in Competitive Markets in the Irkutsk Oblast in Summer 2000

Town	No of firms	Minimum price observed	Maximum price observed	Mean	Price span	Ratio max to min
Taishet	17	3.8	4.6	4.1	0.8	1.20
Bratsk	16	5.5	6.36	5.87	0.86	1.15
Sayansk	14	4.38	6.00	5.01	1.62	1.36
Tulun	14	4.00	4.97	4.48	0.97	1.24
Nizheneudinsk	14	3.6	4.92	4.39	1.32	1.37
Kutulik	6	3.43	3.43	3.43	0	1
Irkutsk	6	3.86	4.69	4.27	0.83	1.21
Sima	4	4.38	6.69	5.25	2.31	1.52
Yurti	4	3.8	4.2	4	0.4	1.10
Lesogorsk	4	4.5	5	4.6	0.5	1.11
Osa	3	3.09	4.5	3.79	1.41	1.45

Source: Survey 2000

6.3.2 Determinants of Prices

As already mentioned the expected determinant for price is market structure, i.e. the number of firms in the market and the concentration ratio. Furthermore, it was already argued that an integration of markets is expected within markets and between neighboring markets. However, the discussion above revealed important reasons why these relations cannot be established in the present context. The following regression model determines the average prices in the markets.

$$price = \beta X_i + \varepsilon$$

where β is a parameter vector and X are explanatory variables. The distribution of the error term is assumed to be bivariate normal. The regressors are described below:

- **Herfindahl index *(HI)***: As a low concentration ratio indicates high competition in the market the relation is expected to be positive. However, in the present context, market relations are assumed to be distorted and hence, the HI is expected to show weak impact on average prices.
- **Total number of firms in the market** (*Tofirm*): For the total number of firms the same argument applies as for the HI.
- **Distance to the next bakery** (*distance*): This variable stands for the integration between markets. Hence, if integration between markets is present, short

distances to neighboring bakeries lead to lower average prices in the respective markets.

- **The presence of a market oriented new bakery** (present=1, not present=0; *Clu1*): This variable as well as the following variable additionally stands for the competition in the market. If market oriented bakeries or bread plants are present it is expected that prices are more likely to be higher because of the cost plus argument explained above.
- **The presence of an old bread plant** (present=1, not present=0; *Clu4*)

Table 6-9 shows the regression results. As the sample size is small (87 observations) several models are presented where HI and Tofirm are included alternatively. The results indicate that market structure shows no influence on average prices. Distortions can also be assumed in the functioning of competitive markets. However, the results confirm that the presence of market behavior has an influence on prices in the sense that higher prices are more likely to appear if market oriented firms are present. Furthermore, some kind of territorial integration of prices can be concluded, i.e. neighboring bakeries are likely to place prices at the same price level.

Table 6-9: Estimation on Average Price; Model: OLS

	Model 1	Model 2	Model 3	Model 4	Model 5	Model 6
HI	-.1657245 (.3595778)	.1390809 (.3638207)	.5626982 (.4108831)			
Tofirm				.0465785* (.0271748)	.0066928 (.033832)	-.0102418 (.0345379)
Distance	.0075863 (.2723216)	.0090107* (.004859)	.0110467* (.0047487)	.0087305* (.0046951)	.0097455* (.0046258)	.0126998* (.0046657)
Clu1		.6672506* (.2598774)	.6165361* (.253833)		.5965928* (.3127685)	.5965928* (.3071723)
Clu4			.5202569* (.2268821)			.5994458* (.2137968)
Number of observations	63	63	55	63	63	55
Adjusted R squared	0.0045	0.0894	0.1886	0.0476	0.0877	0.1596
F	1.14	3.03	4.14	2.55	2.99	3.56

Source: Survey 2000, author's own calculations

6.4 Summary

This chapter dealt with the third aspect of organization of an industry during transition as derived in chapter three. It could be shown that market oriented and non-market oriented new bakeries are spatially separated in terms of their presence in local markets. The presence of market oriented and non-market oriented bakeries in the same market is rather seldom. Hence, since non-market oriented bakeries are almost exclusively located in rural areas, it can be concluded that rural areas are isolated from market development.

Furthermore, the description of enterprise types within single markets revealed that in large urban markets in the center a smaller number of new bakeries has emerged, while in towns more distant from the center huge numbers of new bakeries have emerged which leads to competition in these markets. Though it cannot be proved from evidence in the surveys, it provides grounds for the supposition that entry barriers are posed on the side of the administration.

The rules of market structure that have been proved for the driving school industry in Sweden, which is comparable to the bread industry, have not been repeated in the analysis conducted. Neither a relation between firm size and market size nor equal firm size distribution within markets could be found. While a market-structure-market-size relation has been found in the correlation for all enterprises, this relation broke down in a selected correlation and in the regression model. Furthermore, a relation between market structure and price formation could not be established statistically. Only a relation between the price formation of market oriented and non-market oriented bakeries could be found.

Hence it follows that competition and markets have partly developed and are spatially separated from locations with market imperfections, but even in the developed markets distortions, for example in the functioning of the price mechanism, can be shown.

7. Summary and Conclusions

7.1 Problems Studied and Contributions

While research on transition has contributed to an enormous extent to questions at the macro-level or to questions on reallocation, profitability and efficiency across industries, and recently on labor markets, less attention has been paid to the transition of single industries. However, the study of single industries allows insights into crucial questions of market development, for example on the development of entrepreneurship and its role in the development of markets and for the reallocation of production in old Soviet enterprises. The study contributes to the questions of enterprise development and reallocation in a single industry by studying the bread industry in the Irkutsk Oblast in Russia.

Furthermore, the study aimed at contributing empirically to the new strand of theories developing under the framework of spatial economics. Though the theoretical discussion had already started fifteen years ago, it has found little expression in empirical studies so far. Again, many studies have been published across sectors, and therefore miss important aspects of the spatial organization of industries. For the present dissertation the spatial dimension served as a tool to detect imperfections in market development and to make the segmentation of market development and possible non-market development more distinct.

Chapter three discusses theoretically the spatial organization of the example industry, bread production, in a planned economy and in a market economy setting. However, the expected changes during transition are not derived in a comparative static manner from this discussion. Distortions in the economy that have emerged during transition, or that stem from Soviet times but have strengthened during transition, as well as the existence of the planned economy production pattern, are identified as important factors for the development of markets and integrated into the discussion of hypotheses. Three basic aspects have been identified that need to be studied to contribute to the question of 'How much market has developed?'. That is the process of emergence of new bakeries, the description of the enterprise population at an assumed end stage of the transition process, and the analysis of the markets themselves.

7.2 Summary of Findings

In chapter three the hypothesis was drawn that old enterprises remain in the market as part of the 'virtual economy' while new enterprises emerge that lead to a dispersion of bread production in the region. This is the development that has been found in the study region. Hence, chapter four was dedicated to the analysis of the emergence of the new entities over time. The process of emergence of new bakeries has been studied in the theoretical framework of innovation diffusion. The spatial aspect in this part of the study is represented in two ways. It was hypothesized that two diffusion mechanisms overlie each other of which one is very quick and shows a rural-urban dimension, while the other can be represented by a normal diffusion process which is related to the distance to the economic centers of the region.

While a descriptive model that combines the two processes has been proved by the actual observations in the region, the detection of determining factors has been less definite. While demand factors and the rural-urban dimension have been identified as determining factors, the transition factors could not be detected that unambiguously. The distance to economic centers as a factor that represents the diffusion process does not show impact but the distance to neighboring bakeries explains where the next bakery emerges. That transition factors were less significant than the market factors for the emergence of new bakeries is still plausible as in a demonetized economy there is still demand for bread, which has to be met. However, this does only reflect the emergence of bakeries as demand driven but does not necessarily mean that the new enterprises are market oriented and that the markets are functioning.

To detect the market orientation of the enterprises, in chapter five a cluster analysis of the new enterprises was conducted that should reveal different types of enterprises. Unexpectedly the analysis revealed only two groups of enterprises. However, these could unambiguously be designated market oriented and non-market oriented enterprises according to almost all studied indicators. Market oriented enterprises, on average, emerged later than non-market oriented bakeries which is in compliance with the hypotheses derived in chapter three. Furthermore, they are almost exclusively located in rural areas while market-oriented enterprises are to a larger extent located in urban areas. Nevertheless, they can also be found in rural areas. The goals the bakeries of the different groups pursue are different: while the group of market oriented enterprises wants to make profits and serve demand, non-market oriented enterprises want to provide their workers with bread. Market oriented enterprises are significantly larger by number of workers and produce a much broader assortment of products than non-market oriented bakeries. Furthermore, they have to a much larger extent widened their assortment over time, and hence have developed their businesses. They partly show influence from competition and demand, which the non-market enterprises deny entirely. The non-market oriented enterprises produce on the basis of their own grain while the market-oriented enterprises almost entirely use bought inputs. Furthermore, the non-market oriented enterprises are to a much larger degree involved in barter transactions, particularly in payment in kind to their workers. Hence, the new enterprises are divided into two groups, of which one is affected by transition phenomena and the other is not. Furthermore, these groups are spatially segmented in the sense that one group is exclusively located in rural areas while the other is mainly located in urban areas.

According to the criteria studied, the old bread plants show results that are similar to the results of the market oriented enterprises. They face strong competition from new bakeries and have adjusted their assortments and reorganized their marketing channels. Single plants have downsized. However, the size of some of the old plants is remarkable and indicates 'virtual economy'. The production facilities of the additional system in the rural areas do not show particularly clear results according to the indicators. They have partly adjusted to markets while, given some indicators, others are still run like planned economy facilities.

The third aspect of the transition of a single industry is the development of markets, i.e. the market structure and the relations within and between the markets. The reallocation that was expected to occur according to chapter three at the same time reveals the spatial aspect of industrial organization. It was expected that the production of bread would disperse over space while old enterprises remain and build a dominant firm with a fringe in the urban markets. This is the development that has been found in the region. Spatial reallocation has occurred only through new enterprises; large old bread plants have neither closed down nor moved to other locations. Hence, a huge number of monopoly markets in rural areas has emerged while competitive markets have emerged in urban areas. Nevertheless, the size of the market explains neither the existence of a bakery in the market nor the market structure where bakeries have been observed.

Large enterprises in urban markets in the center and in urban markets at a distance from the center face different situations of competition. Large plants in towns distant from the center are under higher pressure to adjust in order to compete with new bakeries while fewer competitors have entered the central markets and compete with old enterprises.

With regard to the spatial dimension, the results of chapter four have been repeated in chapter six. The most important dimension is the urban-rural dimension, which at the same time answers the question 'How much market has developed?'. Roughly, it can be stated that, according to the developments in the bread industry, markets have developed in urban areas while in large parts of the rural areas markets have not developed. The average distances between bakeries is 27 km which is at the lower limit of possible distances assumed by the planners. Furthermore, the enormous increase in locations show that the planners had been far from meeting their goals. Hence, the spatial organization of the industry has adjusted even towards planned economy results. It follows that distance is an important factor for the organization of an industry. That is supported by the fact that the distance to the next bakery is significant for the emergence of bakeries.

However, the markets in the urban areas show certain peculiarities that indicate malfunctioning of the markets. Besides the above-mentioned distortion of the market-size-market-structure relation, the structure within markets, i.e. the size distribution of enterprises, shows that an organization of markets has developed that is unexpected for functioning markets. Moreover, the analysis of prices reveals the same malfunctioning. While a common price level with bakeries in neighboring locations could be detected, the price span within markets is wide. Regarding the rural-urban dimension, it was found that the price level of non-market oriented bakeries is lower, as expected in the hypothesis derived in chapter three, and hence a relation of decreasing prices with increasing market fragmentation cannot be detected. Nevertheless, it has been shown that the price levels in the markets tend to be higher with increasing distance to the next market.

Still, the emerged market structures are as expected and, furthermore, the relation between old and new enterprises shows that competition has been introduced. The reports of old enterprises on competition show that the emergence of small businesses is crucial for the adjustments of strategies and production decisions of old enterprises, and that it fosters competition. The location of old enterprises that face strong competition and the presence of a high number of small bakeries in these markets are correlated. Furthermore, the presence of small bakeries in urban markets increases with increasing distance from the center. The changes in the assortments of plants and bakeries show that competition leads to adjustments towards the requirements of the customer. However, the development of innovative products in the region in the year 2000 was still limited.

7.3 Overall Conclusions

The findings show that the question 'How much market has developed?' was valid. Though the dispersion of new bakeries over space was demand related, functioning markets have not developed in all cases. Three different areas of action can be identified.

The best examples of functioning markets are towns that lie distant from the center where large numbers of new bakeries have emerged that successfully compete with large enterprises. Though these towns represent the form of development of markets that could have been expected in the best case, the malfunctioning, for example the enormous price spans within markets, show that improvements can still be achieved. These markets are already on the way to functioning markets. The development of new entrepreneurship, particularly in a fragmented industry like bread production, is crucial for the continuation of the process The means for this lie in a better access to small credits for small enterprises, in the reduction of administrative hurdles that hinder diversification and make development of small business undertakings expensive, but also in the development of management skills. This seems to be very crucial as the number of new bakeries that study their markets is very low, and the information on which they base their operations is far from being complete.

While this applies to all market oriented bakeries, the situation of entrepreneurs in the central market seems to be more complex. The best management skills do not help if there is no access to markets. The analysis could not detect the barriers to entry as they were not named by the enterprises as such. However, in the central region few bakeries have emerged though the largest markets are located there. From their absence it can be guessed that high barriers to entry exist which can be related to connections between administration and management of old bread plants.

The most problematic and complex situation reigns in parts of the rural areas where the absence of bread markets is only a symptom. As bread is a basic good it can be concluded that few other businesses emerge in these areas. Here even a 'so far' added to the question 'How much market has developed?' does not apply. In the case of rural areas a solution for the problems is not a matter of time and learning processes. The isolation of market development is rooted in the demonetization of the region and a subsequent vicious circle. However, bringing money alone to the areas cannot solve this. A sustainable market development is only possible on the basis of profitable agricultural enterprises which pay their workers and create demand in the areas. In the peculiar case of rural areas in Siberia with extremely low population density the question has to be brought up whether these areas can be preserved at all.

8. References

Abed, T. A. & H. R. Davoodi, 2000. *Corruption, Structural Reforms, and Economic Performance in the Transition Economies.* IMF Working Paper, WP/00/132.

Aidis, R., 2002. *Why Don't We See More Small- and Medium-sized Enterprises (SMEs) in Lithuania?.* Tinbergen Institute, Discussion Paper 2002-038/2. Amsterdam.

Amemiya, T., 1985. *Advanced Econometrics.* Harvard University Press, Cambridge.

Andersen, B., 1999. The Hunt for S-shaped Growth paths in Technological Innovation: A Patent Study. *Journal of Evolutionary Economics,* 9: 487-526.

Andersson, A., Batten, D. F. & Ch. Karlsson, 1989. *Knowledge and Industrial Organization.* Springer-Verlag: Heidelberg.

Anselin, L., 1986. *Spatial Econometrics: Methods and Models.* Dordrecht Boston London: Kluwer Academic Publishers

Applegate, H., 1994. The Economic Impact of New Firms in Post-Socialist Countries: Bottom Up Transformation in Eastern Europe: A Review Article. *Small Business Economics,* 6 (5): 397-402.

Aslund, A., 1999. *Why has Russia's Economic Transformation been so Arduous?.* Washington DC: World Bank.

Asplund, M., 1998. *On the Size Distribution of Firms and Markets.* SSE/EFI Working Paper Series in Economics and Finance No. 288. Stockholm.

Asplund, M. & R. Sandin, 1997. 'Competition in interrelated markets: An empirical study'. *International Journal of Industrial Organization,* 17 (3): 353-369.

Audretsch, D. B., 1994. Small Business in Industrial Economics: The New Learning. *Revue d'Economie Industrielle,* 67 (1): 21-39.

Backhaus, K., Erichson, B., Wulff, P. & R. Weiber, 1994. *Multivariate Analysemethoden.* Berlin, Heidelberg, New York: Springer-Verlag.

Bain, J., 1954. Economies of Scale, Concentration and Entry. *American Economic Review,* 44 (1): 15-39

Bartoloni, E. & M. Baussola, 2001. The Determinants of Technology Adoption in Italian Manufacturing Industries. *Review of Industrial Organization,* 19: 305-328.

Baptista, R., 2000. Do Innovations Diffuse Faster within Geographical Clusters? *International Journal of Industrial Organization*, 18: 515-535.

Berkin, N. S., Filippowa, S. A., Boyarkin, W. M., Naumowa, A. M. & G. W. Rudenko, 1993. *The Irkutsk Oblast. Natural Conditions in the Administrative Raions (Irkutskaya Oblast. Prirodnye Usloviya Administrativnykh Rayonov)*. Irkutsk: University of Irkutsk.

Brezinski, H., Franck, E. & M. Fritsch, 1998. *The Microeconomics of Transformation and Growth*. Cheltenham & Northhampton: Edward Elgar.

Broadman, H., 1999. *Russian Enterprise Reform: Policies to Further the Transition*. Washington: World Bank.

Broadman, H. G. & F. Recanatini, 2001. *Is Russia Restructuring? New Evidence on Job Creation and Distruction*. Washington: World Bank.

Brock, G. J., 1999. Exploring a Regional Technical Efficiency Frontier in the Former USSR. *Economics of Planning*, 32: 23-44.

Brown, A. & J. D. Brown, 1998. *Does Market Structure Matter? New Evidence from Russia*. SITE Working Paper No. 130, Stockholm.

Brown, A.N., Ickes, B.W. & R. Ryterman, 1994. *The Myth of Monopoly: A New View of Industrial Structure in Russia*. World Bank. Policy Research Working Paper, 1331.

Brown, J. D. & J. S. Earle, 2000. *Competition and Firm Performance: Lessons from Russia*. SITE Working Paper No. 296, Stockholm.

Brown, L. A., 1981. *Innovation Diffusion. A New Perspective*. London and New York: Methuen.

Business Karta (Agency for Business Information), 1999. *Volume Eight: Food Industry: Bread and Rolls, Cakes and Pastries (Pishtshevaya Promyshlennost: Khleb, Khlebobulochnye Isdeliya, Muchnye Konditerskiye Isdeliya)*. Moscow: Business Karta.

Chang, R. & A. Velasco, 1999. *Liquidity Crises in Emerging Markets: Theory and Policy*. NBER Working Paper, No. 7272.

Chavance, B. & E. Magnin, 1995. The Emergence of Various Path-dependent Mixed Economies in Post-Socialist Central Europe. *Emergo*, 2 (4): 55-75.

Chavas, J.-P., Cox, Th. L. & E. Jesse, 1998. Spatial Allocation and the Shadow Pricing of Product Characteristics. *Agricultural Economics*, 18 (1): 1-19.

Chepurenko, 1998. *The Russian Small Enterprises in the Second Half of the 90ies. Part One: Development, Achievements, Problems (Die Russischen Kleinunternehmen in der Zweiten Hälfte der 90er Jahre. Teil 1: Entwicklung, Leistung, Probleme)*. Berichte des Bundesinstitutes für Ostwissenschaftliche und Internationale Studien. Köln: Bundesinstitut für Ostwissenschaftliche und Internationale Studien.

Cheung, F.K. & X. Wang, 1995. Spatial Price Discrimination and Location Choice with Non-uniform Demands. *Regional Science and Urban Economics*, 25: 59-73.

Christaller, W., 1993. *The Central Settlement in Southern Germany. An Economic-geographical Study on the Regularity of Distribution and Development of Settlements with Urban Functions (Die Zentralen Orte in Süddeutschland. Eine Ökonomisch-geographische Untersuchung über die Gesetzmäßigkeit der Verbreitung und Entwicklung der Siedlungen mit Städtischen Funktionen)*. Jena.

Comittee for State Statistics of the Irktusk Oblast, 1997. *Statistical Book on the Administrative-territorial Division - Population (Statisticheskiy Sbornik Administativno-territorialnoye Deleniye Chislennost Naseleniya)*. Irkutsk.

Comittee for State Statistics of the Irktusk Oblast, 1998. *The Industry of the Irkutsk Oblast in the Year 1997 (Promyshlennost Irkutskoy Oblasti v 1997 godu)*. Irkutsk.

Comittee for State Statistics of the Irktusk Oblast, 1999. *Food Processing Industry of the Irkutsk Oblast 1998 (Pishtshevaya Promyshlennost Irkutskoy Oblasti v 1998 godu)*. Irkutsk.

Comittee for State Statistics of the Irktusk Oblast, 2000. *Socio-economic Situation in the Towns and Districts of the Oblast (Sozialno-ekonomitcheskoye Polozheniye Gorodov i Rayonov Oblasti)*. Irkutsk.

Commander, S. & Ch. Mumssen, 1998. *Understanding Barter in Russia*. EBRD Working Paper, No. 37. European Bank for Reconstruction and Development.

Coombs, R., Saviotti, P. & V. Walsh, 1987. *Economic and Technological Change*. Macmillan Education: London.

Council for the Study of Production Forces at GOSPLAN USSR (SOPS) 1971. *Technical-economic Indicators for the Allocation of Food Industry (Tekhniko-ekonomicheskiye Pokasateli dlya Rasmeshtsheniya Pishtshevoi Promyshlennosti)*. Moscow.

Council for the Study of Production Forces at GOSPLAN USSR (SOPS) 1972. *Complex Problems of the Allocation of Agricultural Production and Food Processing Industry (Kompleksniye Problemy Rasmeshtsheniya Selskokhosyaystvennogo Proisvodstva i Pererabatyvayushtshey Promyshlennosti)*. Moscow.

Council for the Study of Production Forces at GOSPLAN USSR (SOPS), 1984. *Problems of Rational Allocation of Meat and Milk Processing Enterprises (Problemy Razionalnogo Rasmeshtcheniya Predpreiyatiy po Pererabotke Myasa i Moloka)*. Moscow.

Council for the Study of Production Forces at the GOSPLAN USSR (SOPS), 1989. *Fostering the Efficient Use of the Production Potential of the APK (Povysheniye Proisvodstvennogo Potenziala APK)*. Moscow.

Council for the Study of Production Forces at GOSPLAN USSR (SOPS), 1992. *Methodological Questions on the Forecasting of the Territorial Development of the APK under the Circumstances of Emerging Market Production (Metodicheskiye Woprosy Prognosirovaniya Territoriyalnogo Rasvitiya APK pri Formirovanii Rynka Prodovolstviya)*. Moscow.

Degras, J. & A. Nove, 1964. *Soviet Planning. Essays in Honour of Naum Jasny*. Oxford: Basil Blackwell.

Desai, P. & T. Idson, 1998. *To pay or Not to Pay: Managerial Decision Making and Wage Withholding in Russia*. Columbia University: Discussion Paper.

Desai, P. & T. Idson, 1998. *Wage Arrears, Poverty, and Family Survival Strategies in Russia*. Columbia University: Discussion Paper.

Deutsche Telekom AG, 2001. Yellow Pages 2001/2002. Koeln: Grevens Adress-buchverlag.

Donckels, R. & A. Miettienen (ed.), 1997. *Entrepreneurship and SME Research: On its Way to the Next Millennium*. Aldershot Brookfield USA Singapore Sydney: Ashgate.

Earle, J.S. & Z. Sakova, 1999. *Entrepreneurship from Scratch: Lessons on the Entry Decision into Self-employment from Transition Economies*. SITE Working Paper, 145. Stockholm.

Eber, N., 1997. A Note on the Strategic Choice of Spatial Price Discrimination. *Economics Letters* 55: 419-423.

Eckes, Th. & H. Rossbach, 1980: *Clusteranalysen*. Stuttgart, Berlin, Koeln, Mainz: Kohlhammer.

Elsner, K., 2000. *Analysing Russian Food Demand Using Micro-Data*. Proceedings of EAAE IX Congress: 342-380.

Ericson, R. E. (2002): *The Russian Economy*. Columbia University, Department of Economics, Discussion Paper 0102,07. Columbia.

Ericson, R. E. & B. W. Ickes, 2000. *A Model of Russia's "Virtual Economy"*. BOFIT Discussion Papers, 10, Helsinki.

Estrin, S. & A. Rosevear, 1999. Enterprise Performance and Ownership: The Case of Ukraine. *Journal of Comparative Economics*, 27 (3): 442-458.

Everitt, B. S., 1993. *Clusteranalysis*. London, Sydney, Auckland: Arnold.

Fakin, B., 1997. Investment-decision Criteria and Resource Allocation in Transition. *Economics of Planning*, 30 (1): 17-31.

Felder, St. & H. Brinkmann, 2002. Spatial Allocation of Emergency Medical Services: Minimizing the Death Rate or Providing Equal Access?. *Regional Science and Urban Economics* 32 (1): 27-45.

Forsyth, J., 1992. *A History of the Peoples of Siberia*. Cambridge, New York, Port Chester, Melbourne, Sydney: Cambridge University Press.

Frohberg, K. & P. Weingarten, 1999. *The Significance of Politics and Institutions for the Design and Formation of Agricultural Policies*. Halle: Institut für die Agrarwirtschaft in Mittel- und Osteuropa.

Frohberg, K., Schulze, E. & P. Tillack, 2001: Factors Determining Profitability of Large Scale Farms in the Volgograd Region. *Quarterly Journal of International Agriculture*, 40 (1): 67-96.

Fujita, M., Krugman, P. & A. Venables. 2000. *The Spatial Economy*. Cambridge, Massachusetts, London: The MIT Press.

Furubotn, E. G., 2000. *Institutions and Economic Theory: The Contributions of the New Institutional Economics*. University of Michigan Press: Ann Arbor.

Gaddy, C. & B.W. Ickes, 1999. *Stability and Disorder: An Evolutionary Analysis of Russia's Virtual Economy*. The Davidson Institute Working Paper Series, 276, Ann Arbor.

Gaddy, C. & B.W. Ickes, 1999. An Accounting Model of the Vitual Economy in Russia. *Post-Soviet Geography and Economics*, 40 (2): 79-97.

Gaddy, C. G., 1998. 'Russia's Virtual Economy'. *Foreign Affairs*, 77 (5): 53-67.

Geroski, P. A., 2000. 'Models of Technology Diffusion'. *Research Policy* 29 (4/5): 603-625.

Ghosh, A. & G. Rushton, 1987. *Spatial Analysis and Location-Allocation Models*. New York: Van Nostrand Reinhold Company.

Gottinger, H. W., 1991. Adoption Decisions and Diffusion: Implications for Empirical Economics. *Schweizerische Zeitschrift für Volkswirtschaft und Statistik*, 127 (1): 17-34.

Greene, W. H., 2000. *Econometric Analysis*. New Jersey: Prentice-Hall Inc.

Grigoryeva, A. A., 1983. *The Economic Geography of the Irkutsk Oblast (Ekonomitcheskaya Geografiya Irkutskoy Oblasti)*. Irkutsk: University of Irkutsk.

Guriev, S. & B. W. Ickes, 1999. *Barter in Russia*. Working Paper.

Hägerstrand, Th., 1967. *Innovation Diffusion as a Spatial Process*. Chicago: University of Chicago Press.

Hancock, K.-E., Holden, D.-R. & J.-K. Swales, 1991. Consistency of the Spatial Allocation of NHS Hospital Resources: An Econometric Analysis. *Applied Economics* 23 (10): 1623-1636.

Hartmann, M. & J. Wandel, 2001. *Food Processing and Distribution in Transition Countries: Problems and Perspectives*. Studies on the Agricultural and Food Sector in Central and Easter Europe 13. Kiel: Wissenschaftsverlag Vauk Kiel KG.

Heckman J. J., 1979. Sample Selection Bias as a Specification Error. *Econometrica*, 47 (1): 153-167.

Hirshleifer, J., 1984. *Price Theory and Applications*. New Jersey: Prentice-Hall Englewood Cliffs.

Hsu, S. K. & L.-T. Tan, 1999. Agroindustry Location under Output Price Uncertainty. *The Annals of Regional Science*, 33 (3): 289-303.

International Bank for Reconstruction and Development, 2002. *Transition: The First Ten Years. Analysis and Lessons for Eastern Europe and the Former Soviet Union*. Washington DC: World Bank.

Ioffe, G. & T. Nefedova, 1997. *Continuity and Change in Rural Russia. A Geographical Perspective*. Colorado and Oxford: Westview Press.

Isard, W., 1956. *Location and Space-Economy: A General Theory Relating to Industrial Location, Market Areas, Land Use, Trade and Urban Structure*. New York: MIT Press.

Ishmuratov, B. M. & L. L. Kalen (ed.), 1999. *Natural and Organisational-economic Resources of Agriculture in the Preangarsk. (Prirodnye i Organisazionno-ekonomitsheskie Resursy Selskogo Khosyaystva Priangarya)*. Irkutsk: Russian Academy of Science. Sibirian Department. Institute of Geography.

Julien, P.-A., 1993: Small Businesses As A Research Subject: Some Reflections on Knowledge of Small Businesses and Its Effects on Economic Theory. *Small Business Economics*, 5 (2): 157-166.

Kalugina, Z., 1998. *Paradoxes of the Agrarian Reform in Russia*. Novosibirsk: Institute of Economics and Industrial Engineering.

Kalugina, Z. (ed.), 1996. *The Sibirian Village in the Transformational Period of Social-economic Relations (Sibirskaya Derewnya v period Transjormazii Sozialno-ekonomicheskikh Otnosheniy)*. Novosibirsk: Russian Academy of Science. Siberian Department. Institute of Economics and Industrial Engineering.

Kalugina, Z. I. & I. N. Martynova, 1994. *Off-Formal Labor in the Russian Agrarian Sector*. Novosibirsk: Institute of Economics and Industrial Engineering.

Kamps AG. 2001. Annual Report 2000. (www.kamps.de/menu/frame2.html)

Kapur, S., 1995. Technological Diffusion with Social Learning. *The Journal of Industrial Economics*, 43: 173-195.

Khryshtsheva, A. T. (ed.), 1997. *Economic and Social Geography of Russia. (Ekonomitsheskaya Geografia Rossiya)*. Moscow: Kron-Press.

Kirilenko, A. S., 2000. *Economic Problems of Food Production in the Irkutsk Oblast (Ekonomicheskiye Problemy Prodovolstvennoy Basy Irkutskoy Oblasti)*. Irkutsk: Publication Centre Journal 'Sibir'.

Klüter, H. & E. Giese, 1990. Territoriale Produktions-Komplexe in der Sowjetunion (Territorial Production Complexes in the Soviet Union). *Geographische Rundschau*, 42 (7/8): 396-401.

Klüter, H. & E. Giese, 1990. Industrielle Erschließung und Entwicklung Sibiriens (Industrial Exploitation and Development of Siberia). *Geographische Rundschau*, 43 (9): 386-395.

Konrad, K. A., 2000. Spatial Contests. *International Journal of Industrial Organization*, 18: 965-974.

Kontorovich, V., 1988. The Process of Organizational Innovation in a Command Economy. *Journal of Institutional and Theoretical Economics*, 144 (5): 878-884.

Kornai, J., 1995. *Das Sozialistische System. Die Politische Ökonomie des Kommunismus*. Baden-Baden: Nomos Verlagsgesellschaft.

Krelle, W., 2000. *Problems of Transition from a Planned to a Market Economy*. Bonn Econ Discussion Papers No. 4/2000. Bonn: Graduate School of Economics.

Krieger-Boden, Ch., 1995. *The Spatial Dimension in Economic Theory. Elder and Newer Approaches to Explanation (Die räumliche Dimension in der Wirtschaftstheorie. Ältere und neuere Erklärungsansätze)*. Kiel: Institut für Weltwirtschaft.

Kuhn, A., 2001. *Trade Costs and Regional (Des-) Integration (Handelskosten und Regionale (Des-) Integration)*. Frankfurt am Main: Peter Lang – Development Economics and Policy, 21.

Kuhn, A. & P. Wehrheim, 1999. Classification of the Russian Regions with Particular Consideration of Agriculture and Food Economy (Klassifizierung Russischer Regionen unter Besonderer Berücksichtigung der Agrar- und Ernährungswirtschaft). *Europa Regional*, 7 (2): 2-9.

Kurzew, I.W., 1996. *The Economy of the Siberian Agro-Industrial Complex in Transition to Market Economy (Ekonomika Agropromyshlennogo Kompleksa Sibiri v Period Perekhoda k Rynochnym Otnosheniyam)*. Novosibirsk: Russian Academy for Agroscience, Siberian Department.

Kurzew, I.W. (ed.), 1995. *Organisational-economic Foundations of the Formation and Development of the Multifaceted Economy of Siberia's APK (Organisazionno-ekonomitsheskiye Osnovi Formirovanniya i Rasvitiya Mnogoykladnoy Ekonomiki APK Sibiri)*. Novosibirsk: Russian Academy of Agricultural Science Sibirian Department.

Kwoka, & White, 2001. The New Industrial Organization and Small Business. *Small Business Economics*, 16 (1): 21-30.

Levitsky, J. (ed.), 1996. *Small Business in Transition Economies. Promoting enterprises in Central and Eastern Europe and the former Soviet Union.* London: IT Publications.

Lifanchikov, A.N. (ed), 1983. *The Food Industry of Siberia and the Far East. (Pishtshevaya Promyshlennost Sibiri i Dalnevo Vostoka).* Moscow.

Lim, H. & C. R. Shumway, 1996. Profit Maximization, Returns to Scale, and Measurement Error. The Review of Economics and Statistics. 74 (3): 430-437.

Lösch, A., 1939. *Die Räumliche Ordnung der Wirtschaft (The Economics of Location).* Jena.

Lundgren, N. G., 1996. Bulk Trade and Maritime Transport Costs: The Evolution of Global Markets. *Resources Policy*, 22 (1-2): 5-32.

Martin, D., Senior, M.-C. & H.-C.-W.-C. Williams (1994). On Measures of Deprivation and the Spatial Allocation of Resources for Primary Health Care. *Environment and Planning* 26 (12): 1911-1929.

McIntyre, R. J., 1998. Building Real Markets under Conditions of Policy Chaos: Russian Regional Strategies and Chinese Precedents. *Emergo*, 5 (4): 53-70.

Melyukhina, O. & P. Wehrheim, 1996. *Russian Agricultural and Food Policies in the Transition Period: Federal and Regional Responsibilities in Flux.* Discussion Papers Food Economy and Food Policy, Series: The Russian Food Economy in Transition, 5. Institut für Ernährungswirtschaft und Verbrauchslehre, Lehrstuhl für Ernährungswirtschaft und Ernährungspolitik, Christian-Albrechts-Universität Kiel.

Merkulov, P. I., 1997. *75 Years Bread Industry. Beginning and Development - Trouble and Hope (Otrasli Khleboproduktov - 75 lyet. Stanovleniye i Rasvitiye. Trevogi i Nadyozhdi).* Moscow.

Nijkamp, P. (ed.), 1986. *Handbook of Regional Economics.* Amsterdam: North-Holland.

Nove, A., 1977. *The Soviet Economic System.* London Boston Sydney: George Allen & Unwin.

Nove, A. & A. Zauberman, 1964. *Studies on the Theory of Reproduction and Prices. Problems of Economic Theory and Practice in Poland.* Warszawa: PWN - Polish Scientific Publishers.

OECD, 1999. *Financing Newly Emerging Private Enterprises in Transition Economies.* OECD Proceedings.

OECD, 1997. *Russian Federation.* OECD Economic Surveys.

Parr, J. B. & J. K. Swales, 1999. 'Competition and Efficiency in a Spatial Setting'. *Journal of Regional Science,* 39 (2): 233-243.

Parr, J. B. & J. K. Swales, 1996. 'Industry Cost Curve and the Spatial Organization of Production'. *Scottish Journal of Political Economy,* 43 (3): 301-316.

Pfirrmann, Oliver, 2002. *Small Firms and Entrepreneurship in Central and Eastern Europe: A Socio-Economic Perspective.* Heidelberg: Physica-Verlag.

Quaim, M., Braun, J. von & H. tho Seeth, 1997. *Food Consumption in Russia. Econometric Analyses with Household Data.* Discussion Papers Food Economy and Food Policy, Series: The Russian Food Economy in Transition, 8. Institut für Ernährungswirtschaft und Verbrauchslehre, Lehrstuhl für Ernährungswirtschaft und Ernährungspolitik, Christian-Albrechts-Universität Kiel.

Rogers, E., 1962. *Diffusion of Innovations.* New York: Collier-Macmillan.

Roland, G., 2000. *Transition and Economics. Politics, Markets, and Firms.* Cambridge, Massachusetts, London: The MIT Press.

Roland, G., 1990. On the Meaning of Aggregate Excess Supply and Demand for Consumer Goods in Soviet-type Economies. *Cambridge Journal of Economics*, 14 (1): 106-150.

Romanov, A.E., 1998. *The Management of APK in Theory and Practice. (Teoriya i Praktika Upravleniya APK).* Moscow, Minsk: Armita.

Rumer, B., 1984. *Current Problems in the Industrialization of Siberia.* Berichte des Bundesinstituts für Ostwissenschaftliche und Internationale Studien, 48. Köln.

Sasaki, K. & S. Kuhinisa, 1995. Evaluation of Road Capacity and its Spatial Allocation. *Annals of Regional Science* 29 (2): 143-154.

Schmalensee, R. & R. Willig, 1989. *Handbook of Industrial Organization.* Amsterdam New York Oxford Tokyo: North-Holland.

Schroeder, G. E., 1989. The Implementation and Integration of Innovations in Soviet-Type Economies. *Cato Journal*, 9 (1): 90-118.

Schwalbach, J., 1994: Small Business Dynamics in Europe. *Small Business Economics*, 6 (1): 21-25.

Serova, E. & I. Khramova, 2000. *Emerging Supply Chain Management in Russia's Agro-Food Markets.* Discussion Paper: The Russian Food Economy in Transition, No. 14. Zentrum für Entwicklungsforschung. Bonn.

Serova, E. & N. Karlova, 2000. *Liberalization and Decentralization in a Transitional Economy: Regional Disintegration of the Russian Agrifood Sector. The Case of Eastern Regions of Russia.* Working Paper. Institute for the Economy in Transition. Analytical Centre Agrifood Economy. Moscow.

Serra, D., ReVelle Ch. & K. Rosing, 1999. 'Surviving in a Competitive Spatial Market: The Threshold Capture Model'. *Journal of Regional Science,* 39 (4): 637-652.

Shaw, D. J. B., 2000. *Russia in the Modern World.* Oxford Malden: Blackwell Publishers.

Sheng, M., 1997. *Consumption Analysis for Russia: A Linear Expenditure System.* Discussion Papers Food Economy and Food Policy, Series: The Russian Food Economy in Transition, 12. Institut für Ernährungswirtschaft und Verbrauchslehre, Lehrstuhl für Ernährungswirtschaft und Ernährungspolitik, Christian-Albrechts-Universität Kiel.

Shotski, V. P., 1979. *Agro-Industrial Complexes and Types of Agriculture in Eastern Siberia.* Budapest: Akadémiai Kiadó.

Shy, O., 1998. *Industrial Organization.* Cambridge, Massachusetts, London: The MIT Press.

Slider, D., 1997. 'Russia's Market-distorting Federalism'. *Post-Soviet Geography and Economics,* 38 (8): 445-460.

Stadelbauer, J., 1996. *Die Nachfolgestaaten der Sowjetunion. Grossraum zwischen Dauer und Wandel (The Soviet Union's Successor States: A Major Region between Continuity and Change).* Darmstadt: Wissenschaftliche Buchgesellschaft.

Stiglitz, J. E., 1999. *Whither Reform? Ten Years of the Transition.* Paper for the World Bank Annual Bank Conference on Development Economics.

Sutton, J., 1991. *Sunk Costs and Market Structure.* Massachusetts, London: The MIT Press Cambridge.

Sutton, J., 1997. One Smart Agent. *Rand Journal of Economics,* 28: 605-628.

Syssoeva, N. M., 2001. 'Influence of Demand Potential on the Spatial Structure of Prebaikalski Region Farming Industry in the Transition Period'. *Geography and Natural Resources,* Siberian Branch of the Russian Academy of Sciences Novosibirsk: 106-111.

Tan, L.-T., 2000. 'Welfare-maximizing and Profit-Maximizing Agroindustry Location: A Comparison'. *The Annals of Regional Science,* 34 (1): 69-82.

tho Seet, H., 1995. *Rußlands Haushalte im Transformationsprozeß (Russia's Housholds in the Transition Process).* Frankfurt am Main: Peter Lang.

Tirole, J., 1998. *The Theory of Industrial Organization.* Cambridge, Massachusetts, London: The MIT Press.

Thünen, J.H. von, 1875. *The Isolated State with Regards to Agriculture and National Economy (Der Isolierte Staat mit Beziehung auf Landwirtschaft und Nationalökonomie).* Berlin.

Vashtshanov, V.A., Maslennikova, E.V. & E.N. Borisova, 1995. Structural Organization of the Processing Branches of the APK. (Strukturnyie Preobrasovaniya v Pererabatyvayushtshikh Otraslyakh APK). Ekonomika, 4: 65-74.

Vickrey, W., 1964. 'Spatial Competition, Monopolistic Competition and Optimum Product Diversity.' *International Journal of Industrial Organization*, 17: 953-963.

Wandel, J., 2000. *Landwirtschaft und Industrie in Rußland – der Transformationsprozeß in der Ernährungsindustrie. Eine Analyse im Lichte des Structure-Conduct-Performance-Ansatzes*. Studies on the Agricultural and Food Sector in Central and Easter Europe 10. Kiel: Wissenschaftsverlag Vauk Kiel KG.

Weber, A. 1909. *Über den Standort der Industrien (About the Location of Industries)*. Tübingen: J.C.B. Mohr.

Wehrheim, P., Frohberg, K., Serova, E. & J. von Braun, 2000. *Russia's Agro-Food Sectors. Towards Truly Functioning Markets*. Dordrecht Boston London: Kluwer Academic Publishers.

Wehrheim, P., 2002 (forthcoming), Modeling Russia's Economy in Transition.

Wein, N., 1999. *Sibirien (Siberia)*. Gotha und Stuttgart: Klett-Perthes.

Wildner, S., 1997. *Ernährungssituation und deren Determinanten in Russischen Haushalten im Transformationsprozeß (Nutrition and its Determinants in Russian Households during the Transition Process)*. Discussion Papers Food Economy and Food Policy, Series: The Russian Food Economy in Transition, 10. Institut für Ernährungswirtschaft und Verbrauchlehre, Lehrstuhl für Ernährungswirtschaft und Ernährungspolitik, Christian-Albrechts-Universität Kiel.

Wiles, P. J. D., 1964. *The Political Economy of Communism*. Oxford.

Windhorst, H.-W., 1983. *Geographische Innovations- und Diffusionsforschung (Geographical Research on Innovation and Diffusion)*. Darmstadt: Wissenschaftliche Buchgesellschaft.

World Bank, 2002. *Transition – The First Ten Years: Analysis and Lessons for Eastern Europe and the Former Soviet Union*. Washington D.C.: World Bank.

Appendix 1

Spatial Development of Consumer Markets in Siberia

Questionnaire

The analysis of food processing enterprises is part of a research program on the problem of market emergence for consumer goods in Russia. The survey is designed to collect information on the intra-regional development of consumer markets in the Irkutsk Oblast.

Answering the questionnaire does not take more than one hour. The interviewer will explain all aspects that are not comprehensible to you. In our opinion the results of the analysis of the market situation will be useful also for your business activities. Therefore, we would like to ask you to spend that much time for the interview. If you wish so we will report the results of the analysis concerning your industry to you.

You may resist answering any questions you do not want to answer. In the case of rejection we ask you to give reason for the rejection choosing one of three options: I do not want to answer; I do not know; the phenomenon does not exist. Information is collected only for scientific purposes. The publications, which include a report to the administration of the Irkutsk Oblast, will communicate data on your company only in aggregate form. The interviewer will give you any information on the conducting organization (Institute of Geography, SO RAN) and the coordinator of the survey.

On the questionnaire only the code of the enterprise will appear. A list that combines the code and the name of the enterprise remains in the Institute with the coordinator. We suppose correctness of the subsequent specifications of answers in the process of data analysis and therefore, ask you for the permission to address you again.

Number Code 1	
Specialization	
Town/Village (Raion)	

Date	
Interviewer Code 0	

At the beginning we would like to ask you for some general information on your enterprise.

1. What is the organizational and legal form of your enterprise:
   State enterprise ☐
   Municipal enterprise ☐
   Joint stock company, open type ☐
   Joint stock company, closed type ☐
   Limited liability company ☐
   Co-operative ☐
   Small business ☐
   Other ☐

2. When was your enterprise founded? ___________

3. Could you please tell the reasons for opening a bakery?

   ____
   ____
   ____

4. Which factors determined the choice of location?

   ____
   ____
   ____

Produce

5. Please tell the basic type of products and the number of assortment you produced in 1999.

Type of product	Number of sorts

6. Did you widen or reduce your assortment after starting your business?

widened	☐	***continue with question 7***
reduced	☐	***continue with question 7***
no	☐	***continue with question 9***

7. Please name the products you added to or removed from your assortment

Added

Type of product	Number of sorts	Year

Removed

Type of product	Number of sorts	Year

8. Please describe briefly why you changed the assortment?

____

____

____

9. Please indicate the inputs and the respective amount you used in 1999.

Input:				
t				

10. Please give the three most important products in your assortment and give the respective share in your turnover in 1999.

Commodity:			
%			

11. Please indicate the output of these products in physical units for the year 1999.

Commodity:			
Unit			

12. Please describe the dynamics of production of your bakery since the beginning of the business by help of indicators. If indicators are not available please describe the dynamics of your production verbally.

1990	
1991	
1992	
1993	
1994	
1995	
1996	
1997	
1998	
1999	

Prices

13. The following table shows different commodities. Please give the prices for the products at the 26.06.00 and 10.07.00 in case you produce these products.

Bread (higher sort)	
26.06.2000	
10.07.2000	
Bread (first sort)	
26.06.2000	
10.07.2000	
Bread (second sort)	
26.06.2000	
10.07.2000	
Baton	
26.06.2000	
10.07.2000	
Roll	
26.06.2000	
10.07.2000	

14 Please describe how often the prices for your products change.

____

____

____

15 Please indicate on a five-point-scale from insignificant (1) to significant (5) the importance of the given factors on your price formation.

	Significance				
	Lowest		Middle		Highest
Prices for raw materials and inputs	1	2	3	4	5
Demand	1	2	3	4	5
Competitor prices	1	2	3	4	5
Selling location	1	2	3	4	5

Raw material source

16. Please indicate the sources for your raw materials

Bought grain

Source	Share (%)
Milled outside	
Milled in own mill	

Bought flour	

Own grain

Source	Share (%)
Milled outside	
Milled in own mill	

17. Please name the locations where you purchase flour and mark the cell of the respective partner at this location. If your partners are located in Eastern Siberia please name the district or town, if your partners are located outside Eastern Siberia please name the oblast, krai or republic. In the case of imports please name the country where you buy flour.

	Location:	Location:	Location:	Location:	Location:
Mill					
Middlemen					
Trader					
Wholesale					

18. Please estimate the share of each location, where you buy flour, in the total volume of purchase.

Location:					
Share (%)					

19. Please mark the cell that indicates the respective share of barter transaction in purchasing the given inputs. If you do not have the information to answer precisely please briefly describe the role of barter in your purchasing transactions.

	No barter	< 10 %	11-20 %	21-30 %	31-40 %	41-50 %	51-60 %	61-70 %	71-80 %	81-90 %	91-100 %
Raw material											
Other materials											
Packaging											
Water, electricity											
Services for the selling of production											
Services for transportation											
Services for maintenance and repair											
Payment in kind with workers											

___

___

___

20. Please estimate the stability of relations with your suppliers and indicate the respective share in your transactions.

Relation	Occasional	1-3 years	3-5 years	5-10 years	more than ten years
%					

Marketing Channels

21. Please indicate the location where you sell your production and the partners at these locations. If the partners are located in Eastern Siberia name the town or district please. Indicate the cell that names the respective type of buyer of your production in the locations.

	Location:	Location:	Location:	Location:	Location:
Retail					
Public Catering					
Own retail facilities a) stationary b) mobile					
Middlemen					
Other					

22. Could you please indicate the approximate share of each location in the total volume of your sales in 1999.

Location:			
Share (%)			

23. Could you please indicate the approximate share of each marketing channel in the total volume of your sales in 1999.

Marketing Channel:					
Share (%)					

24. Estimate the share of barter transactions in selling your production, please.

No barter	< 10%	11-20 %	21-30 %	31-40 %	41-50 %	51-60 %	61-70 %	71-80 %	81-90 %	91-100 %

25. Do you take unit price for your products at different selling locations?
Yes ☐
No ☐

26. Do you face problems selling at certain locations?
Yes ☐ ***continue with question 27***
No ☐ ***continue with question 29***

27. Could you please describe these problems?

____
____
____

28. Could you estimate the losses deriving from these problems?
________________(in % of turnover)

29. Please indicate on the five-point-scale from insignificant (1) to significant (5) to which degree the geographical scope of your business activities has changed since the start of your enterprise.

insignificant				significant
1	2	3	4	5

Market Information

30. Could you please briefly describe the way you collect information about your product markets (please also indicate the intensity of collection)

____
____
____
____

Transport

31. Please indicate the share of each mean of transport you employ for purchasing purposes (sum = 100%).

Own transport	Rented transport	Delivery by the supplier	Carrier	Other

32. Please give the share of each transportation mean that you employ for selling purposes (sum = 100%).

Own transport	Rented transport	Collection by the customer	Carrier	Other

33. Please indicate the approximate share of transportation costs that are covered by your enterprise and by your partners for purchasing transactions.
Enterprise ________%
Partner ________%

34. Please indicate the approximate share of transportation costs that are covered by your enterprise and by your partners for selling of your production.
Enterprise ________%
Partner ________%

35. Do you use packaging for the transportation of your production?
Yes ☐
No ☐

Main competitors

36 Who are your main competitors? Please indicate on a five-point scale the significance of different types of enterprises as your competitors from insignificant (1) to significant (5).

	Problem				
	No		Middle		High
Local enterprises (located in the same district)	1	2	3	4	5
Enterprises located in neighboring districts	1	2	3	4	5

Technology

37. Please give the following information on your equipment:
When did you get the equipment you are producing with now? (If you purchased gradually indicate the period, please)
Was the equipment new at the point in time you got it?
In which country was the equipment produced?

Production line	Year	New	Where from?
		Yes ☐ No ☐	
		Yes ☐ No ☐	
		Yes ☐ No ☐	
		Yes ☐ No ☐	

38. Is your equipment in compliance with modern requirements in terms of maintenance of equipment, quality of production and packaging?
Yes ☐
No ☐, continue question
☐ subject to replacement
☐ requires modernization

39 What is the share of actions in the production process done by:
a) hand ______________ %
b) mechanically ______________ %
c) electric means ______________ %

Capacity utilization

40. Please indicate the capacity of your enterprise in the three most important groups of products.

Product group:			
T / shift			

41. Please, indicate the capacity utilization in your enterprise.

	The enterprise practically does not work	less than 30%	30-50%	50-75%	More than 75%
Main products					
Other products					

42. Did you widen the capacities of your enterprise since the beginning of your activities?
    Yes ☐
    No ☐

43. Do you plan to widen your capacities of your enterprise in the next twelve months?
    Yes ☐ ***continue with question 44***
    No ☐ ***continue with question 45***

44. The production of which products do you plan to expand?

    ____

    ____

45. Do you develop a business plan?
    Yes ☐
    No ☐

Problems

46. Please explain the most important problems your enterprise faces which
    A) are connected with the location of your enterprise (Please do not name more than three problems)

    ____

    ____

    ____

    ____

    B) are on Oblast or federal level (Please do not name more than three problems).

    ____

    ____

    ____

    ____

47. Please describe where in your enterprise you see scope for improvements and the respective way of solving the problem.

____

____

____

____

Indicators that characterize the location of the enterprise:

48 What is the length and quality of routes to the main communication line?

- ☐ Asphalt km ____________
- ☐ Leveled but unpaved road km ____________
- ☐ Earth road km ____________

49. Water-supply

Type or source	☐	own taking
	☐	municipal net
Sufficiency	☐	sufficient
	☐	not sufficient

50. Electricity-supply

Type or source	☐	departemental station
	☐	power supply system
Sufficiency	☐	sufficient
	☐	not sufficient

51. Telecommunication

Type	☐	telefon
	☐	faks
Sufficiency	☐	no problem
	☐	problems with connection

52. Do you face recruitment problems, if yes, please name the problems

Yes ☐

No ☐

____

____

At the end of the interview we would like to pose some question on financial indicators of the enterprise:

53. How many persons work in your enterprise? __________
    a) Out of these, how many belong to the production force? __________,

    Out of the total production force
    b) Seasonal workers __________,
    c) Part-time workers __________.
    d) Share of qualified personnel __________.

54. Please give the average income paid to your workers

    ____

55. Can you please give the approximate structure of your expenses (%)?

Raw material	Other materials	Electricity, water, gas	Depreciation	Rent	Transport	Marketing facilities	Wages	Other

56. Please give
    a) the turnover for the year 1999 __________
    b) the expenses on production and marketing 1999 г. __________
    c) Your fixed capital at 01.01.2000 (in roubles) __________
    d) Your profit for the year 1999 __________

Appendix 2

Figure 1: Number of Bakeries in the Irkutsk Oblast in 1992

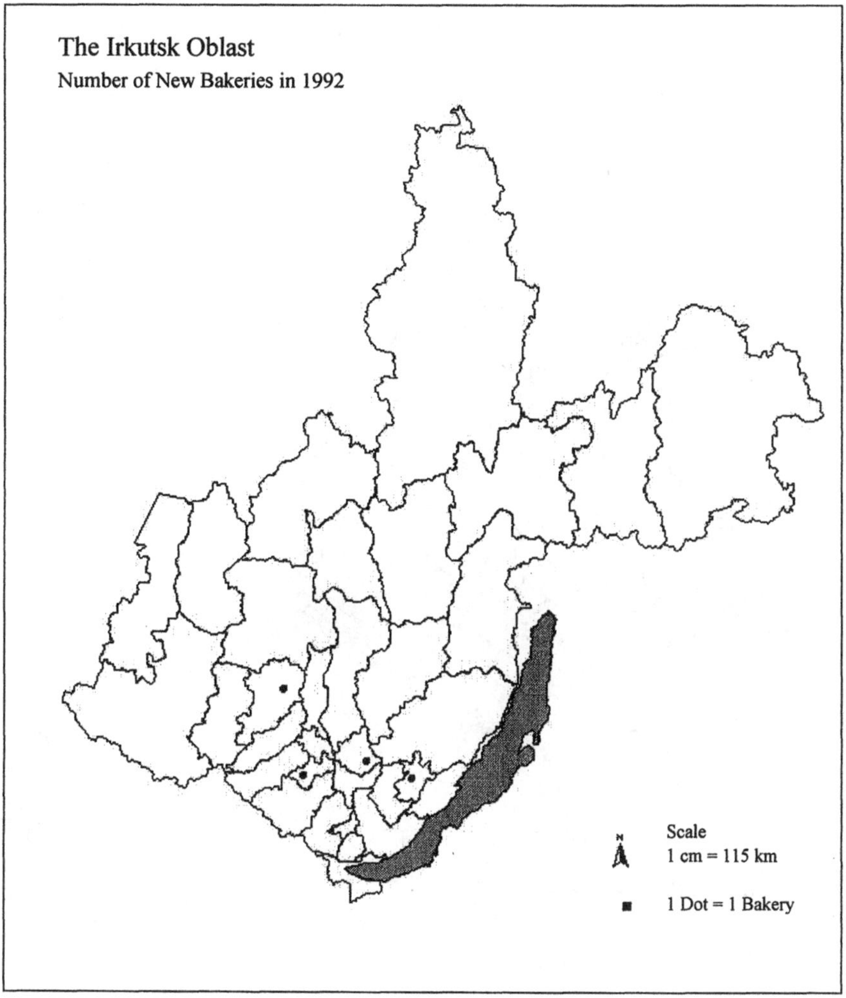

Source: Survey 2000, own drawing

Figure 2: Number of Bakeries in the Irkutsk Oblast in 1993

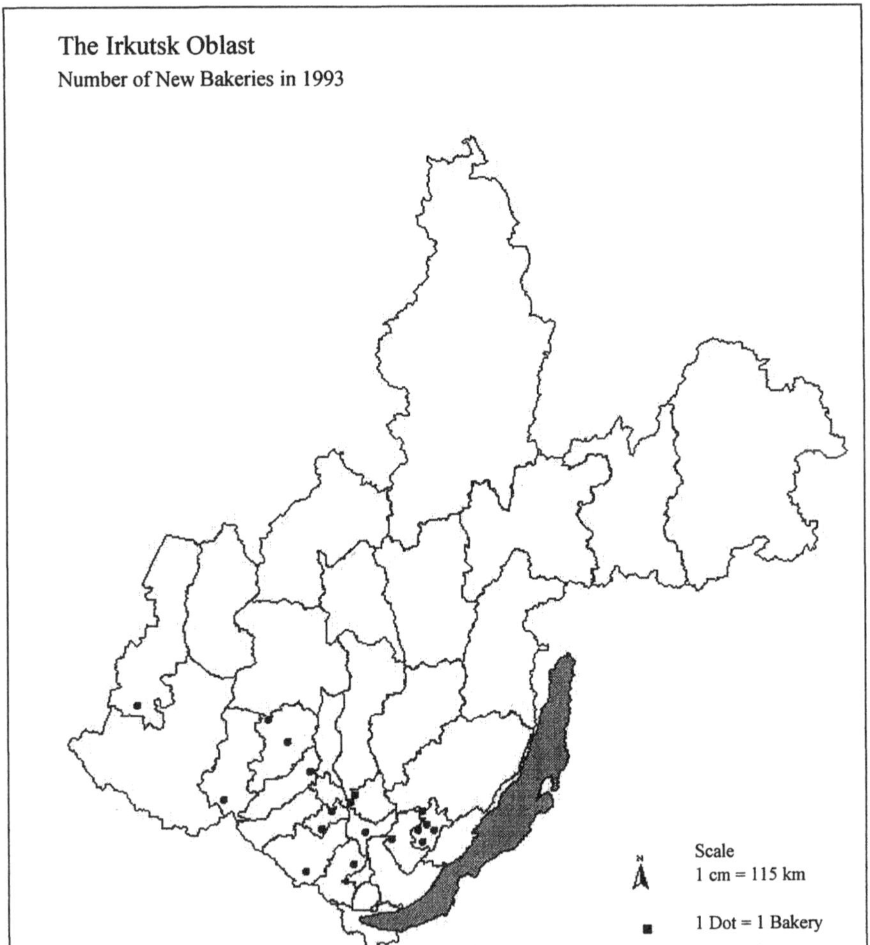

Source: Survey 2000, own drawing

Figure 3: Number of Bakeries in the Irkutsk Oblast in 1994

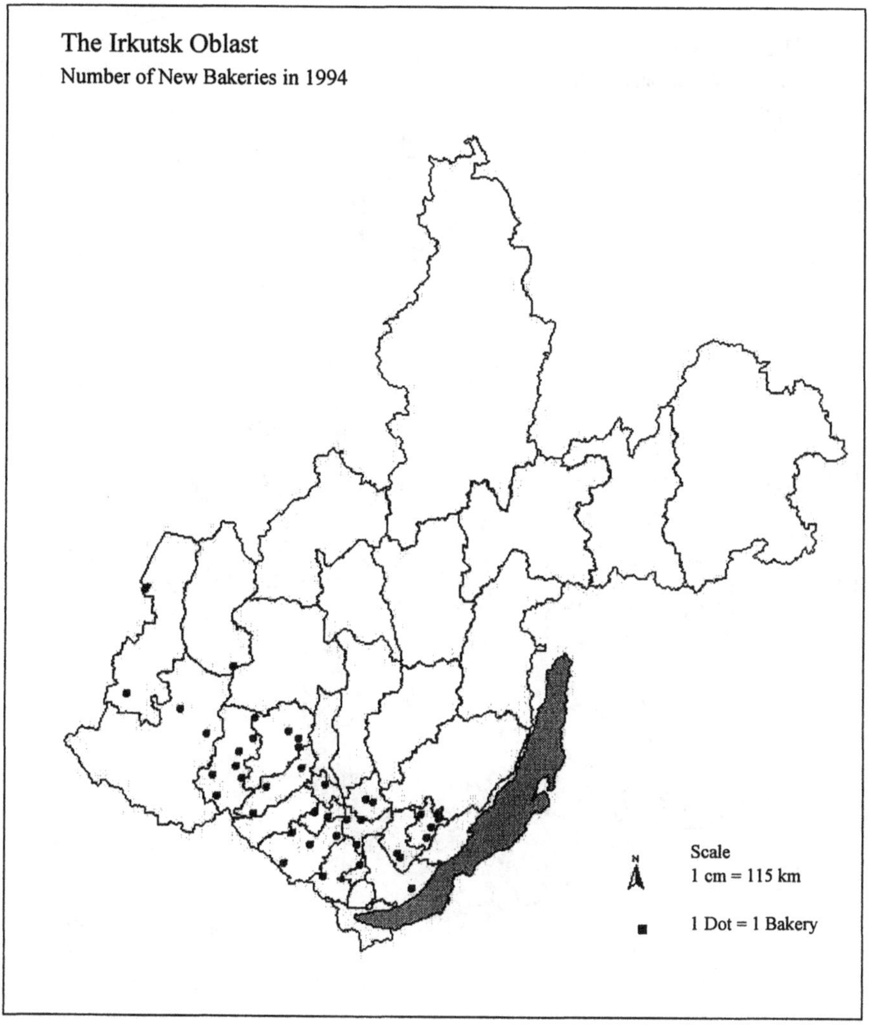

Source: Survey 2000, own drawing

Figure 4: Number of Bakeries in the Irkutsk Oblast in 1995

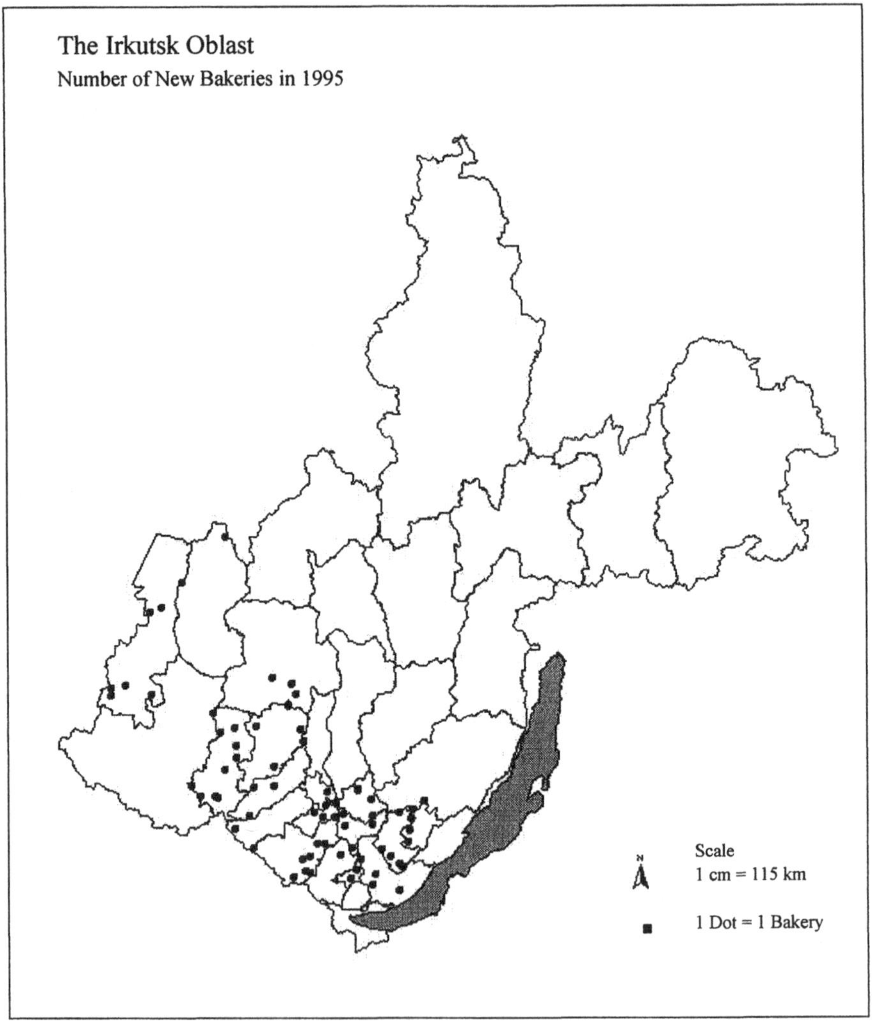

Source: Survey 2000, own drawing

Figure 5: Number of Bakeries in the Irkutsk Oblast in 1996

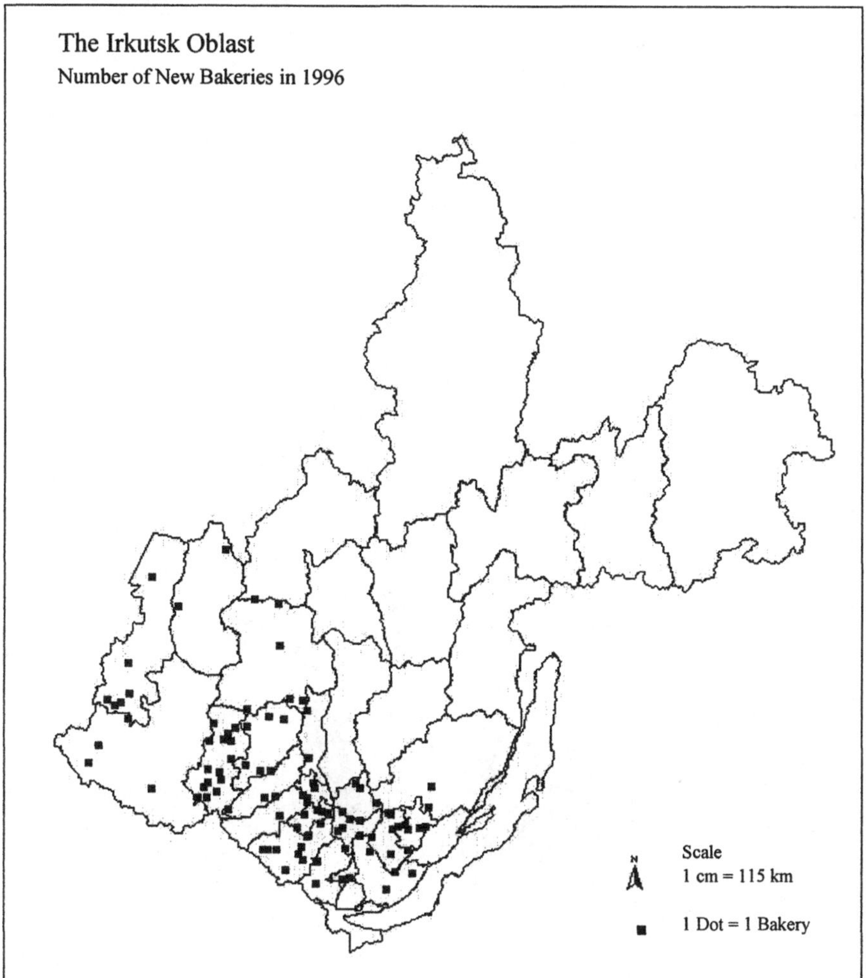

Source: Survey 2000, own drawing

Figure 6: Number of Bakeries in the Irkutsk Oblast in 1997

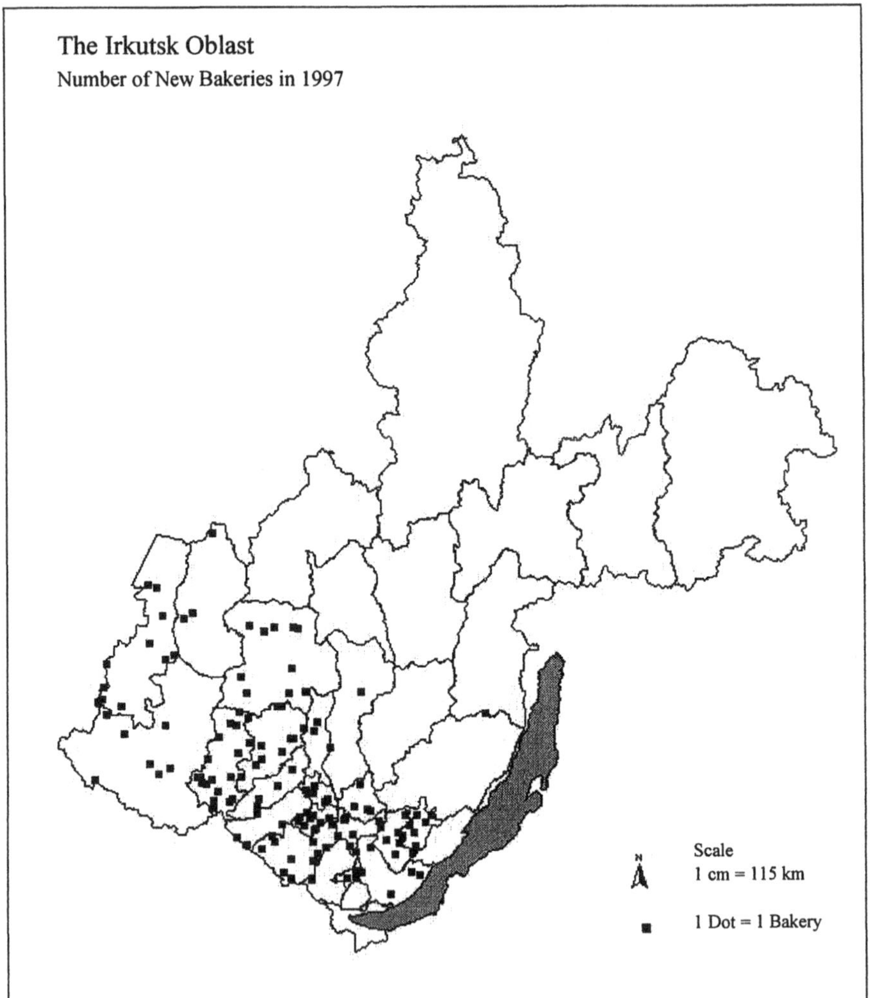

Source: Survey 2000, own drawing

Figure 7: Number of Bakeries in the Irkutsk Oblast in 1998

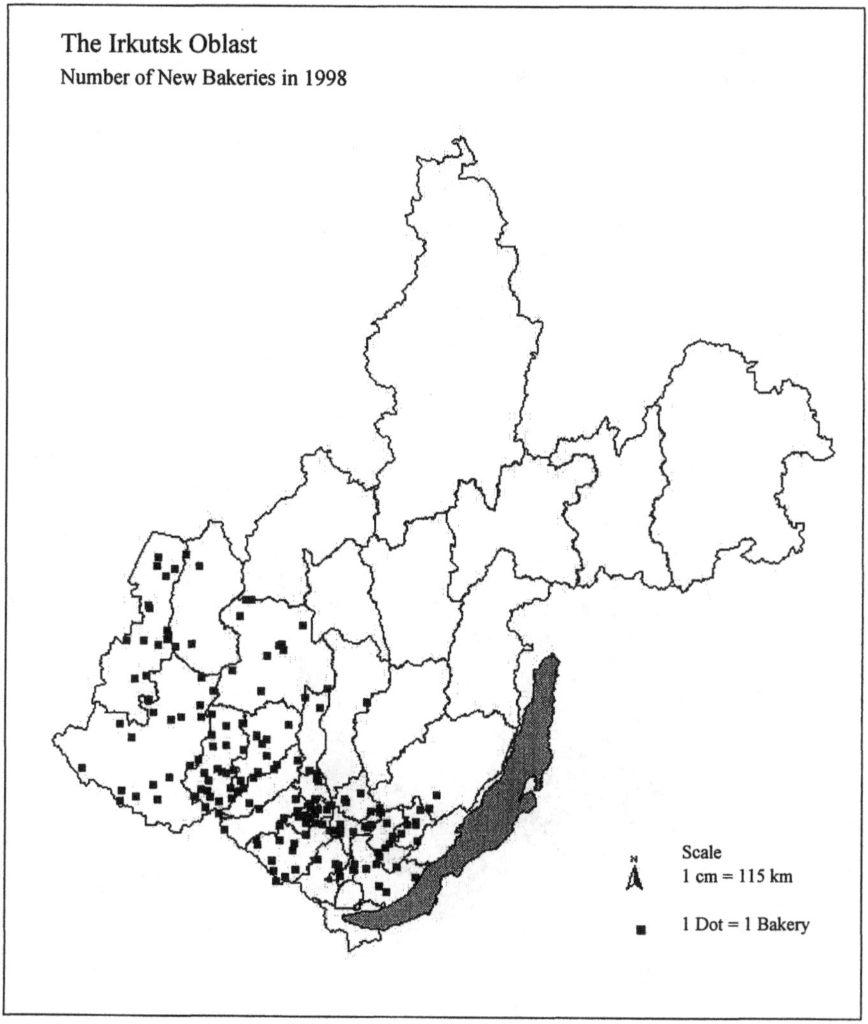

Source: Survey 2000, own drawing

Figure 8: Number of Bakeries in the Irkutsk Oblast in 1999

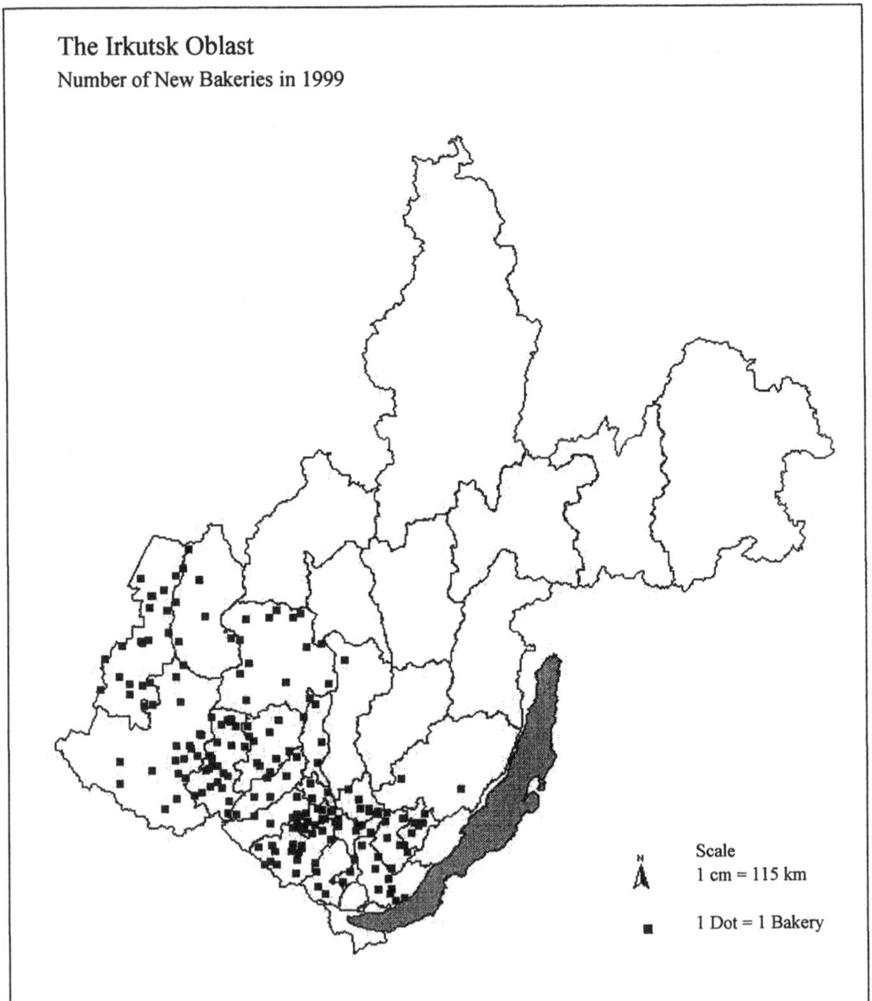

Source: Survey 2000, own drawing

Figure 9: Number of Bakeries in the Irkutsk Oblast in 2000

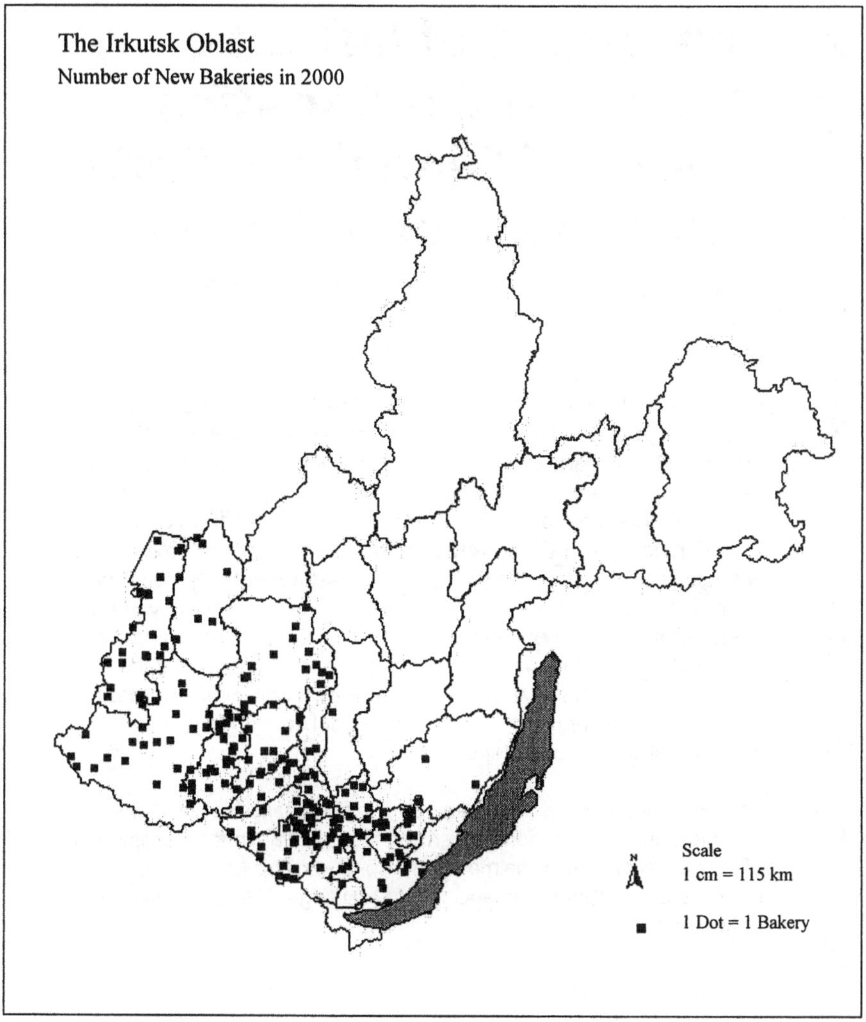

Source: Survey 2000, own drawing

Gertrud Buchenrieder

Sequencing of Institution Building in the Transition Process of Central and Eastern Europe's Financial Systems

Frankfurt am Main, Berlin, Bern, Bruxelles, New York, Oxford, Wien, 2002.
XLIII, 513 pp., num. fig. and tab.
ISBN 3-631-39886-7 / US-ISBN 0-8204-6030-3 · pb. € 86.00*

Few issues in economics have experienced such a grandiose revival as the role of institutions in economic change. With the beginning of the transition process in Central and Eastern Europe and the former Soviet Union, optimal sequencing and timing of reforms in the transformation process became a focus of scholarly research. Clearly, the success of the reform efforts in transition economies depends to a considerable extent on the existence of adequate institutions. Financial systems are institutions. The objective of financial system reforms is to expand the volume and efficiency of financial intermediation. This work analyses the sequencing and timing patterns of structural and institutional reforms in the financial systems and the macro-economic empirical evidence of financial system reforms in six transition countries. These are Bulgaria, the Czech Republic, Hungary, Poland, Romania, and the Slovak Republic.

Contents: Sequencing, timing and building of financial institutions and organisations · Institution sequencing and building in the transition process of a financial system at the macro-, meso- and micro-level · Empirical evidence of institution sequencing and building – The rural financial market in Romania

FSC
www.fsc.org
MIX
Papier | Fördert
gute Waldnutzung
FSC® C083411

Zeitfracht Medien GmbH
Ferdinand-Jühlke-Straße 7
99095 Erfurt, Deutschland
produktsicherheit@kolibri360.de

Druck:
CPI Druckdienstleistungen GmbH
im Auftrag der
Zeitfracht Medien GmbH
Ein Unternehmen der Zeitfracht - Gruppe
Ferdinand-Jühlke-Str. 7
99095 Erfurt